TALES OF THE NEGLECTED HOUSE WIVES

TAMIKA DAVIS

ISBN:
978-1-105-08048-7

ACKNOWLEDGEMENTS

I would like to thank the women who took the time to tell their stories and share them with women everywhere. I always want to thank the God I serve who gives me the strength to do all things. I thank you, God, for giving me the patience and ability to write.

To my husband, children, and family I thank you for your support and encouragement.

I dedicate this book to homemakers everywhere who feel less than appreciated. May God give you the strength to confront and fix the problems in your marriage and live happily ever after!

TALES OF THE NEGLECTED HOUSEWIVES

Marriage can be such a blessing and bring such a sense of pride and accomplishment in a woman's life. Then there are times when you question yourself, what in the world was I thinking? Husbands can really build you up as well as tear you down. The way they treat you, how they speak to and about you, the respect factor, and if they make you feel loved. Some husbands know just what to say and do to make their wives feel like a queen on the throne of his heart. That makes for a happy woman. Then there are the husbands who treat their wives like the trash you find blowing in the wind on city streets. That is a recipe for disaster, and sadly; it seems many women are being treated as such. The one thing that men need to really wrap their heads around is that it doesn't take much to make a woman happy. Women may come in different sizes, shapes, colors, heights, weights, and races but the one thing all women have in common is the need for love and respect. If a man comes home to his wife every day after a hard day's work, embraces her with love, and asks her how her day was she's a happy camper. She then responds with love and proceeds to tend to his needs. She takes his hat and coat and tells him to sit down in his favorite chair. She brings him a cold beverage while he awaits dinner's completion. While he's sipping his beverage she brings his house shoes, takes off his work shoes and socks, and places the slippers upon his tired feet. In that, she is showing reverence to her husband. She is showing him how she appreciates and loves him. The two may share a short conversation before eating dinner, depending on if the man is in the mood for conversation, based on how his workday went. If he initiates conversation, she knows at this point he's in the mood to talk. Now the lines of communication are open and that's important in a marriage. Communication, trust, mutual respect, and love are necessary in a good marriage. So much can go wrong without them.

DEB'S DRAMATIC DUO

I, Debbie Statham, got married on October 20, 1973 to Phillip Peters. None of my family members attended due to a spur of the moment wedding at a local church in Michigan. At first, the marriage was going good and we were happy. Phillip and I like any other married couple wanted to start a family together. A year later, I was pregnant with our first child. Right before the baby was born seems to be when the trouble began. I was about 7 months pregnant when Phillip walked out on me. He never contacted me over the last two months of the pregnancy but he sent $100 a week via mail. When I saw him again it was five days before giving birth. My Aunt Mildred called Phillip and informed him that I had just found out I was having twins. When he walked into the hospital room, he automatically focused on my stomach. He said he couldn't believe there were twins inside. I noticed that Phillip had a bunch of passion marks all over his neck and inquired about whom they came from. Phillip's response was, he was at a party and a bunch of women pinned him down and put them on his neck. Phillip is a chronic liar. He lied about the silliest things and made up outrageous tales about all types of things. I laughed off his silly reply and informed Phillip that I am scheduled for a C-Section today. The funny thing was I went into labor 60 minutes prior to being prepped for my C-Section. The doctor let the labor progress to see how it would go. After 7 hours of labor, I am only dilated 2 centimeters. The doctor went inside and noticed both babies are heading for the birth canal at the same time. At that time, the doctor decided to go ahead with the C-Section before the twins and I reached the danger zone. After the process was over and I gave birth to the twins, I fell out from the drugs they put in my system.

The first three weeks the twins and I resided at my mother's house. Philip and I reconciled at that time. After the three weeks, I moved in with my mother and father in law. I resided there for about 4 months. Shortly after, Phillip and I purchased our first home together, across the street from his parents. Things seemed to be going well for a while. Then about five months down the line Phillip began staying out all times of the night and coming home in the wee hours of the morning. One day I confronted Phillip about his comings and goings and we got into a huge argument. Phillip was getting dressed for work and after he put on his work boots and stayed quiet for a second. I began to turn around and walk away and that's when Phillip kicked me as hard as he could in my lower back with the soul of his boot. I went flying from one side of the kitchen to the other. I hit the counter first and then the ground, hard! Phillip didn't show any signs of remorse or concern about my well being. I pulled myself up slowly and looked back at Phillip with question marks in my eyes. Wondering how could he possibly treat his wife, the mother of his children in such a manner?

Three weeks later, Phillip's older brother, Carroll dropped by for a visit and began grilling Phillip. He was asking him questions that left me feeling somewhat antsy about what's going on. At one point, Carroll turned around, looked me straight in the whites of my eyes and said," He hasn't told you what he's been up to lately has he?"

I replied with a confused look on my face, "What the hell are you talking about Carroll?"

"Oh, he didn't tell you that he's been out of work for the last three weeks? The bastard quit his job at Ford Motors, after our dad worked so hard to get him in."

I stood there with a stunned look on my face. I had no idea he was even out of work being that he wasn't home during the hours he should have been at work. Now the question is, where was he going and staying at all this time when he was pretending to be at work? That fool was wasting time at a local bar when he was supposed to be at work. When he wasn't bringing a check home that peeked my curiosity. When I confronted him, he always had an excuse. He lied and said the computer system that made out the checks at work had some kind of virus in it. So being that there was no income, I had to put the house on the market.

Philip favored one twin over the other. He felt he preferred the one twin who was more like him to the other one. In his little mind, he felt like it was okay to treat one a little more special than the other. We are supposed to love our children equally, and not prefer one to the other because they are more like us. Now being that they were identical twins, I don't know how he felt John looked more like him than Joseph. He would always hold and play with John more than he would Joseph. That really made my blood boil.

Around 1983, things began to get worse and the twins were about 10 yrs old. They could understand what was really going on between their dad and me. I remember finding a huge greeting card under the seat in the car, signed D.R. This was someone he met at work. He was cheating on me with a co-worker of his. After I accused him of cheating, he backhanded me, my body flew back, and my head hit the door. As I was getting up, I saw blood and shortly after I notice, my lip was bleeding and tore. I ran into the bathroom, locked the door and looked at myself in the mirror. I saw my lip hanging. Phillip came running to the bathroom door and began banging and demanding to come into the bathroom. He saw what he had done to me and drove me to the hospital. I had to get 20 stitches in my mouth. The ER doctor asked me what happen but I lied and tried to tell him my husband and I were playing around and he accidentally hit me in the mouth. The doctor told me, he knew I was lying and asked me if I would be safe leaving with my husband. I wanted to tell the truth but didn't dare, afraid of what else would happen due to being honest. It was by the grace of God that CPS didn't come and take my kids away from me. Being hit by a man wasn't new to me, I could stand that; but having my kids snatched away was unbearable. They were all I had left, besides faith that God would one day deliver me from this situation eventually. I was really praying for the sooner rather than later though.

In March of 1985, Phillip came staggering home at 11:00am after being out all night. He was knocking and banging on the door and I let him in. He passed out on the living room floor and just slept. Fifteen minutes later, there was a knock at the door, and it was a woman. When I went to the door and opened it, she demanded to see Phillip as if she was his wife. Therefore, I told her to wait just a moment, closed the door, and went back in to wake Phillip and let him know his lover was at our front door. He jumped up, went to the door, and stepped out on the porch with her. They argued loudly for a few minutes and they both had been drinking. Then next thing I know they both left in their individual vehicles and I didn't see him again until six months later. He just returned to pick up his belongings because when he left, he took nothing but the clothes on his back. We divorced and went our separate ways. Eventually I started dating again and putting myself out there to meet someone new to build a future with. I absolutely refused to let one monkey stop the show. Just because he was a bad man, that didn't mean all men were bad. I'm sure there are still some men left here on God's green earth who didn't use and abuse women just for the hell of it. I was really hoping to find one to spend the rest of my life with.

On January 23, 1988 in the wee hours of the morning, I found myself at Roger's Bar. I didn't want to be there but I had to pick up a girlfriend of mine who was too intoxicated to drive. Being the great friend that I am, I went and retrieved her. While I was there, I met a man named Don and we hit it off. A year later, we got married and I planned to live happily ever after. The first two months we were all over each other like rabbits. I conceived in that second month of our marriage. Don treated me well throughout the pregnancy, but the day I went into labor was a horse of another color. As soon as I gave birth, Don immediately became a true blue jackass! When he looked at our son Ryan, he had the nerve to say, "This baby isn't mine, he looks nothing like me!" I was heartbroken and didn't understand. Things weren't quite the same after that. Don and I were okay for the next 3 years but shortly after he began indulging in drugs. He started to be kind of distant and self-centered. While he was sleeping, he didn't want any noise to be made in the house or he would go nuts. Once I was vacuuming while he was in the bedroom and he came running out into the living room screaming at me. He told me not to clean or do anything that makes noise while he's asleep. Then when Don woke up for the day and sat in front of the television he wouldn't want us talking to him until the commercial breaks. The more he did the drugs the more unattached he became to our son and me. He began to get violent, verbally and physically. He could come and go as he pleased but I couldn't. If I simply said hello to a man he would accuse me of flirting or wanting them. This began to be a routine of his and it was so damn annoying. I couldn't extend a common courtesy to other human beings by saying hello without having a huge argument over it. After while, I figured he must be the one out doing all the cheating and flirting. If one is doing all the accusing all the time, that one is usually the cheater. All I did was go to work, tend to our home and our son. I didn't have time to even think about having an affair. At this point I was pretty much convinced that I was done trying to live happily ever after with this nut job. My first marriage was crazy and this one is as well. If I ever think about getting married a third time, please slap the hell out of me!

At this present day, I am still legally married to Don but that's it. I have no love for him and I wish everyday he would just leave and never come back. I have told him how much I don't want him in my life and how much I want him out of my house. I pay all the bills and rent and he doesn't pay anything, except the cell phone bill. I have to pretty much threaten him to do that! The only way to get him out of my life is to divorce him. Funds are low and none to spare outside of paying rent, utilities, car insurance, and getting gas. Come tax season I really hope I get enough money back to pay for a divorce and I can be rid of Don and start life new. He's a big obstacle in my life for many reasons. My two oldest sons won't have anything to do with me because of Don. I got him out of our lives once in the past but I let him sweet talk his way back into my house and my life. Nothing changed; he still mistreated me and didn't help with any bills. He wouldn't even purchase any food for the house. When he got hungry, he would go to Burger King and get him a Whopper meal; come back and eat it in front of our son and me knowing we were hungry. The bastard wouldn't even offer his own kid a damn fry. How sorry can you be?

Soon Don began being mean and abusive to my child and me. He would call our son Ryan all kinds of names and really killed his self-esteem. At the age of 21, he can recall all the evil and hurtful things his father has said and done to him. Once he hit us both and I had to have him removed and locked up. Instead of my mother in law understanding, she had an attitude with me. She yelled, "How could you have him locked up like that?" She never addressed the fact that he was hitting our son and me and how that was wrong. Being that her husband abused her, you would think she would understand where I was coming from. I know as mothers we love our sons but supporting them in their wrongdoing is just terrible. I have always told my sons to never lay a hand on a woman in that way because women are the weaker vessel. We are here on God's earth to be loved, protected, and taken good care of. I remind them not to do to any other woman what their dad did to me. I refuse to uphold any wrongdoing of my children. I adore them, I would lay down my life for them but wrong is wrong and right is right.

I have two marriages and one divorce under my belt, just praying for one more divorce to make a complete set. I can truly say I have tried and given it my all, but marriage just doesn't seem to work for me. I'm hoping to be happily divorced in the near future because this loveless marriage has really taken a toll on me. I just want peace of mind for the rest of my days here on earth. A Big Mac and fries every now and then won't hurt either.

LINDSAY'S LIFE LESSON

My name is Lindsay Somers and I am 30 years of age. I have a 10-year-old son, who is the only male in my life that has loved me. Jonathan Bo Somers is my only reason for living at this point. My husband, Roderick Somers could care less if I lived or died. I truly thought he loved me when we first got together, and maybe he did but it didn't last long. Roderick was my knight in shining armor who rescued me from a life on the streets. I ran into him one night when I was gathering my belongings because I was being removed from my home. My ex, Thomas, tossed me and my clothes out on the front steps. He threw about a thousand dollars down at my feet and slammed the door behind him. I was dating a high profile attorney for about two and half years. One day he decided he wanted a more mature woman who had the same goals and aspirations in life that he has. I didn't have a degree in anything, just my diploma and my lessons that I learned in everyday life. Thomas took all the keys to the cars and the house so I had to get to a hotel the best way that I could. Therefore, I started walking with my rolling luggage in one hand and hitchhiking with the other hand. I thought my thumb and feet would fall off before I'd get a ride. Long behold, a sleek, black, Mercedes-Benz slowed down to a stop by my side. The passenger side window rolled down and there he was. Caramel complexion, beautiful baby brown eyes, and a pearly white wide smile. He asked me where I was headed and offered me a ride. Oddly enough, I wasn't afraid and I had the strangest feeling that he and I were meant to be. He introduced himself as Roderick Somers, I reciprocated with a hello, and my name is Lindsay Rosenberg. We chat each other up a bit and I filled him in on my dilemma. I needed a job and a place to stay or I'd have to go running back home to mommy. Unlike Dorothy, I wasn't in any rush to go back to Kansas. I love the hustle and bustle of everyday life in the city. The beautiful bright lights that light up the night sky. The thousands of people who were all over the place at all times. Day or night, it was always something to get into. Kansas wasn't anything like New York.

Roderick was a big time Advertising Executive and promised me a job at his office. He had a pool house that he let me occupy until I found a place of my own. He was my ride to and from work most of the time so I didn't have to take a bus, cab, or subway. He was a big help to me from the moment we met. You could say it was kind of a miracle. It is said, that when one door closes a window opens. Well when Thomas slammed the door in my face, Roderick opened the window of opportunity for me. How lucky was I? I felt this was a "Pretty Woman" moment, except for the whole hooker thing. Like Julia Roberts, I am beautiful and witty as well.

After the first year, Roderick and I began to grow closer and closer. He dated other women less and less and found himself moving me from the pool house to the main house. It was officially on! Everywhere we went people couldn't keep their eyes off us. We were hot, like Angelina Jolie and Brad Pitt. Who needs a red carpet when we had all of New York as our backdrop? Life was greater than ever. By the second year, we were married and ready to plan a family. We traveled to exotic places and sailed the Caribbean. Although I was Caucasian, my body was sun kissed by the tropic sun all year round. Roderick's mother is Caucasian and his dad is Jamaican. His complexion is beautiful and his eyes so dreamy. His hair was full and fabulous and his brain is bigger than his bank accounts. He is physically fit and has abs of steel. All the perfect makings of a great husband and future father of my children. I couldn't wait to give him a baby so we could complete our family. Roderick wasn't in too much of a rush to start having babies just yet but he did want children.

Year three rolls around and I'm getting bored with just shopping, going to spas, country club lunch dates with the girls, and decorating our home. I need a change because Roderick isn't falling over himself to spend time with me anymore. The only thing this could mean is there's a new chicken in the barn. You already know, I'm heading to the office to see what's really going on. I wasn't handing my man over on a silver platter to some sleazy secretary trying to get ahead. I know the game and I lost it the first time, but not again. There's nothing worse than a determined, obsessed bitch who wants your life.

I popped up unannounced at the office so neither Roderick nor the secretary would know I was coming. When I walked in I immediately noticed the secretary wasn't at her desk where she belongs. I waltz into my husband's office and find the secretary leaning over his desk with her size double D cup breasts on display. They were going over some paperwork but her position was unnecessary. Therefore, I slam the office door behind me as I walk in. Roderick jumps up from his chair and immediately says, "Hello honey, I didn't know you were stopping by for lunch."

"Obviously darling or I'm sure you would have met me in the lobby. Well, and who might this be darling", I ask?

"Umm...this is my new secretary, Rochelle. Rochelle this is my wife, Lindsay", says Roderick.

Rochelle holds her hand out to me, but of course, I bypassed on the handshake. I told Rochelle to report to her desk because I needed some private time with my husband. I made sure there was no confusion about how I felt about her being there. When she left and closed the door behind her, I lit into Roderick. Of course, he told me I was being ridiculous and insecure. How it was strictly business between him and Rochelle. I am no fool! I know that's how we started and where we are now so I will be watching. I left his office a little flustered. I shot Rochelle a look of death on my way to the elevator and put my Gucci shades back on. Personal note to self, start taking kickboxing classes 4 times a week instead of twice a week. Time to get my game face on because she has the hungry look in her eyes, and I know what that's like. Well, I'm in it to win it. This is not reality TV, this is my life and I will not let her or any other female take my starring role.

When Roderick came home that night, he saw me looking online for plastic surgeons. He told me I was being silly that my body was fine and I didn't need to change a thing. I reminded him how he was drooling over Rochelle's bulging boobs this afternoon. He couldn't deny that one. Roderick took me by the hands and lured me away from the computer, looked into my baby blue eyes, and kissed me passionately. He was trying to distract me from the issue of Rochelle's boobs, and it worked. We made love right there on the office floor. A month later I found out we were expecting. It couldn't have come a better time. I surprised Roderick with the news on Valentine's Day. I wrapped the positive pregnancy test up in a nice box, with red paper and a white bow. While we were out at dinner, we exchanged gifts. He brought me a beautiful diamond necklace. I was very pleased; diamonds are this girl's best friend. I then passed him the box with his gift. I smiled inside with the anticipation of his reaction. Roderick finally unwrapped and opened the box. He picked up the pregnancy test and saw it was positive. I then smiled and said, Happy Valentine's Day Daddy! He was totally surprised and happy. At first, I was a little concerned about what his reaction would be. He wanted kids but I think he wanted the baby later than sooner.

"No wonder you passed on the champagne. I was like, that's odd she loves champagne with strawberries. So, we're having a baby. Oh my goodness, we're having a baby everyone", shouted Roderick to those dining nearby. They raised their glasses and toasted congratulations to us both. It was great! I will never forget this night. Every Valentine's Day will remind me of how I announced my pregnancy to Roderick. The first few doctor's appointment were simple enough. About time the second trimester rolled in Roderick began accompanying me to my prenatal appointments. He heard the baby's heartbeat and he was so very excited. It was wonderful to see his face light up like a kid in FAO Schwarz toy store. The next visit would be for the sonogram. That really knocked his socks off. He had a few ultrasound photos to take to the office and show to his co-workers and Rochelle. Things were going better than ever, until one day Roderick had to go out of town for business. The company had some clients in Los Angeles, California. He would be there for about four days. I wanted to go with him but Roderick didn't think it would be good for me to fly. I told him he was being ridiculous and it would be perfectly fine and that I would get a note from the doctor. He then told me, he wouldn't have time to really spend with me anyway because it would be strictly business. No fun in the sun or enjoying Rodeo Drive this time around. I didn't press the issue, but I sure wish I would have. I didn't know Rochelle would be joining him on this little business adventure. A few weeks later, there was another business trip they had to go on. Of course, about time the third trimester rolled around I definitely couldn't fight him on not flying out of town. This time they were headed to South Beach, Miami. There's nothing but beautiful, half naked, tanned women. I spoke to Roderick and voiced my opinion about how I felt about Rochelle joining him on all these trips. He started running down a list of reasons of why I shouldn't be occupying my thoughts with such nonsense and how nothing is going on between them. I didn't argue with him because I didn't want to get all worked up and end up in the hospital to soon. Once again, my husband kissed me good-bye, told me he loved me, and headed out on his new business venture. At times, all I could think of is how he and Rochelle are having a great time on the beautiful Miami beaches. I don't doubt that he took care of business for the office by day; I just wondered how he spent his nights. Sometimes I try to stay busy in the baby's nursery to take my mind off the negative things. I didn't want our son coming out with any nervous problems because mommy was too hyped up during the pregnancy. At this point, I really missed diving into a delicious, hot, cup of caramel macchiato with an extra shot of espresso. I was drooling over the memory of champagne and strawberries. Eventually my mind drifted back to Miami and what was going on? I haven't heard from Roderick since 2pm and it's now 8pm. So I decide to call him. We chatted for a few minutes and he proceeded to rush me off the phone. He was in so much of a rush he didn't even hit the end call button on his phone. I heard smooth jazz playing and a few other voices in the background. One was definitely Rochelle but the other voice wasn't familiar at all. I stood on the line for about thirty-five minutes listening to them enjoying their dinner and wine. Fifteen minutes later, I heard footsteps that began to fade in the distance. I didn't hear anything for a good forty minutes and almost dosed off waiting. Finally, I heard voices again. Someone was saying how tonight was great as they were walking. I then heard a door open so I guess that person left. Two minutes later I heard Rochelle mention a hot shower and a late night swim. I couldn't believe my ears, I was officially pissed off! I hung up the phone immediately and got myself together. I tried to remain calm for the baby's sake. There wasn't any need of the baby being born premature because his daddy was a jack ass! I called my mother and told her what went down. My parents took the first plane out of Kansas to New York. Roderick came home the day after my parents arrived. He went straight to the office from the airport. He called me before his flight but I didn't answer, and once he landed in New York he called me again. I didn't take any of his calls and I wanted him to worry for a change. Roderick left a message on my voicemail saying he had a meeting at 1:00 this afternoon. While he was at his meeting with a new client, I was at his office firing Rochelle's scandalous ass! I kindly told her to pack up her shit and be gone before things get murderous. She looked surprised to hear that type of threat coming out of my mouth. I told her directly that I would have her beat unrecognizable and left in the gutter for dead. Yes, she was totally pissed and I know she wanted to punch me in the face but I was pregnant and her boss's wife. Moreover, she had no supporting arguments. Although she couldn't hurt me physically without being sent to jail, she found another way to get me. She shows me some footage of a video on her phone. Then she threatened to go public with it if I don't give her a quarter of a million dollars. My body went numb as I watched my husband engaging in a three-some with Rochelle and a strange man. There it was in full color; my husband and another man. Things just went from bad to the worst.

I couldn't even respond to her ridiculous blackmail scheme; I was too busy feeling faint. I saw Roderick getting off the elevator and he saw Rochelle aggressively in my face. He had a very tense look on his face that turned to worry as I begin to fall towards the ground. I could hear him yelling my name and running towards me. The next time I opened my eyes I was in his office surrounded by paramedics. Roderick was holding my hand standing over me. Asking what happen and how I was feeling? At that moment, everything came rushing back to my mind like flooding water. The flashback of Rochelle and I arguing and her showing me that video. That made me sick to my stomach; I sat up and grabbed his garbage pail alongside his desk. I began to vomit at the thought of seeing the man I love being sexual with another man. The paramedics checked me out and made sure the baby and I were fine before they left. When the door closed, I gave Roderick the look of death, grabbed my purse and headed towards the door. He pulled me by my hand and asked what the hell went on between Rochelle and Me. I whirled around, looked him in the eyes and said, No the question is, what went on between you and Rochelle? If you want to know what went on you go ask that bitch and while you are at it stay with her! Don't come home because you are not welcome there Roderick. I changed the locks, my parents are here and I don't want anything to do with you!"

Roderick screamed my name and pleaded with me to just talk to him. He acted as if he had no idea what the hell was going on. I filled him on how Rochelle tried to blackmail me for a quarter of a million dollars not to go public with a video showing him with her and another man. Oh, I wish you could have seen the look on his face; it was priceless and pitiful at the same time. I told Roderick to stay the hell away from me and that he would be hearing from my lawyer. He tried so hard to convince me that this was a onetime thing and he's never been with a man before. I told Roderick, not only did you cheat on me while I was pregnant, but you did it with a man and woman! If it was just Rochelle, I could get over that because shit happens, but you were with a freaking man! Dude, that is so not cool in my world! I had to get out of that office before I commit murder. I left him standing there in his office with tears in his eyes. I could care less about the pain he was in because I had too much of my own to deal with. I was so distraught I had to leave my car in the lot and have his driver take me home. When I finally got in the door, I collapsed in my mother's arms with tears in my eyes. I know she could feel my devastation and pain. I told my parents that Roderick and I are over because he cheated on me. I told them about sleeping with Rochelle but that's it. I didn't go into the blackmail and how he had a man as well. I couldn't dare tell me family and friends that. Do you know how much of a fool I would look like? I cared too much for Roderick to embarrass him like that as well. It was a sad situation for us both, but even sadder for our son. He is an innocent bystander in all this. He's going to be born into a chaotic situation from day one. I don't know what the future held for Roderick as far as Rochelle was concerned. The one thing I did know it that I wasn't giving her a damn dime and if she went public with the video I would have to deal with the repercussions and then move on with my life. I wasn't giving in to a terrorist because that's exactly what she is. I knew she had an agenda from day one. Roderick couldn't see beyond her breasts and his lust so he fell right into the trap she set for his stupid ass. Why is it that men never listen to their wives? You can clearly see a trap being set for them and when you say something, you're being paranoid and insecure. Oh my goodness, if you are even being polite and saying hello to another man that spoke to you first; you're being flirty or sending signals. What kind of stupid crap is that? I'm sure people can see this big ass rock on my finger and if they don't, I let them know; I am very happily married so don't even think about it. Men feel like when they are not in our presence we are out just flirting with every man we come across. H-e-l-l-o...wake up and smell the dumbness! My self-respect is based on me, not my husband being around or not.

Anyway, Roderick and I finally talked and worked something out. He is back at home and being a father to our child but that's as far as it goes. We co-exist in a home that has a man and wife divided. We love and raise our son together and just tolerate one another. At first Roderick didn't want to give me a divorce but after two years he finally agreed to sign the papers. We lived happily divorced as friends and co-parents for a while. Once I decided I wanted to start dating again, Roderick moved to the pool house until he felt he wanted to move. Over the years, we still traveled and showed our son, Jonathan the world. He fell in love with Europe by the time he was five years old. Now that Jonathan is ten years old, Roderick and I explained how mommy and daddy are parting ways. We explained how none of it is because of him and we love him more than life. He was somewhat sad but he knew something wasn't right for the last two years. Daddy was living in the pool house and we were in the main house. Roderick and I were good as friends but anything beyond that just wasn't going to happen. It's one thing when you have to compete with another one, but when it comes to competing with a penis, I bow it gracefully. There's no way I can be in a relationship with a man who loves penis more than I do! It's unacceptable in God's eyes, man may accept it and act like it's okay but it's not! God made man and woman to be together as husband and wife. To love one another, have babies and build families. I thank Roderick for giving me our son Jonathan and I forgive him for hurting me. I also pray for him and I hope that was a onetime thing with that man. I never asked him if he paid Rochelle off and I never saw her again.

In any event, Jonathan and I are doing just fine. I have been dating a man from Kansas, and you can rest assure that I am having him checked out thoroughly. Asking him all kinds of questions to be sure he's strictly into women and isn't curious of what it would be like to have a man. Isn't it ironic? I was doing whatever it took to stay out of Kansas and now I'm dating someone from Kansas. Life can be funny sometimes. I truly don't know where this relationship will go, but you can best believe my heart guard will be up. Love has failed me every time so I'm not delusional in that area anymore. As time goes by, we will see if Mr. Kansas is a prince or a frog.

STUCK ON STUPID

My name is Jan and I am having an affair with my husband. We're sneaking around behind his mistress's back. Her name is Renee and she lives two houses down from me. When she first moved into the neighborhood, I welcomed her warmly. We were together almost every day. Renee would come over for coffee and conversation every morning. While I was laid off from work most of my spare time was spent hanging out with Renee. We were shopping and drinking buddies. My house was her second home.

After while, I got a new job and returned into the working world. The first two weeks, a few of the neighbors had noticed Renee being at my home daily even while I was at work. I didn't make a big deal about it, but that's where I made my mistake. While I was at work, she was sipping coffee and conversing with my husband. I mentioned it to my husband being that it became frequent. Of course, he says I'm making a mountain out of a mole hill. You know how men like to try to make you think you're crazy and over reacting to things. We're just being over sensitive and suspicious for nothing. How many married men you know who hang out with their wives friends while she's at work? Then Renee came to me and was saying how nothing's going on and how she's bored over at her place. I told her that it doesn't look nice that she's hanging at my house all day with my husband while I'm at work and our son is at school. Renee claimed she understood and played it very cool. Silly me, I thought things were straight between Renee and me. She really didn't give a damn about what I was saying. All she did was the same things different place. Instead of Renee spending all her free time at my house with my husband, she had him over her house. Damn, what the hell is wrong with chicks these days. No respect for people's marriages or friendships. Don't get me wrong, Renee isn't the only one to blame, my husband is a willing participant. I know some men are dogs and some women are harlots but damn, do I have to have one of each in my life? I treated this girl like a sister.

Anyway, a mutual friend of Renee and mine has let me know that my husband was spending a lot of time at Renee's place. Therefore, I have a day off but don't let my husband or Renee know. They both think I have to work today. I treat myself to breakfast at Denny's and head back home. When I get home, my husband is nowhere to be found. Therefore, I stroll over towards Renee's place quietly and slowly. I know she leaves her side door open sometimes so I walk to the side of her house. The door is indeed open, I slide inside the house cautiously, with my ears, and eyes wide open. I hear sounds of passion so I follow them to Renee's bedroom. The door is cracked so I peek in and there she is. Bumping and grinding with my husband, Jack. Every fiber of my being wanted to rush in and kill them both, but I didn't. Prison wasn't on my list of places to go and I have a son to take care of. I quietly crept back out the side door, hopped in my car and left. Although I had the day off, I went to my office, got some paperwork done and I even called Jack. I asked him how his day was going and what he did today. Of course, he tells me his day was boring and how he's scanning the want ads looking for work. The fool doesn't know I saw his stupid ass putting in work at Renee's. I told him to go in the fridge, take out the roast, and put it in the oven to bake at 350. At this point I had to focus on what I would do to get even to keep me from blowing up at him.

Later on that evening, I arrived home with a cake for dessert and a smile on my face. Jack greeted me at the door and embraced me. During dinner, he spoke about going to Atlantic City for the weekend. I told him I was all for it. He suggested we invite some of our friends. Why wasn't I surprised? He was setting it up to bring Renee without making it seem so obvious. I'm going to play the game right along with him, but there will be only one winner in the end. There were many weekend getaways to come. Renee and a few other friends joined us many times. This time around, Jack decided he wanted to go down without me. I have been telling Jack that his unemployment will eventually run out and he shouldn't waste money on gambling and drinking. He's using that to start a heated argument and say he needs time alone. No doubt, his time alone will be spent with Renee. The Friday he left Renee was home, she even came over to eat lunch with me. About midnight I watched through my bedroom window as she got in her car and left with an overnight bag. Around 1:30 in the morning, I called her cell phone and asked her if she could come over and sit with my son because I needed to go to the ER. She gave me some song and dance about her being over at mom's place. Yeah okay, as if I don't know she took her ass to Atlantic City to be with Jack. Sunday evening Jack came home and informed me that he was leaving me. Wow! Really wasn't expecting that one. I actually cried and asked him why? I knew we weren't doing that great financially but that's not a reason to end a marriage. I pleaded with him to give our marriage a chance. I asked him if it was me; was I to fat or unattractive in his eyes? Of course he gave me the old, it's not you it's me speech. Jack told me he feels like we've grown apart, that he's interested in someone else, and they're tired of hiding their relationship. Now my blood is really boiling! He's really telling me about how he and his mistress are tired of sneaking around to spare my feelings. Is he truly serious? I knew he was having an affair with Renee but I didn't think it was to the point where he loved her more than me. Twenty minutes later, Renee comes to my door and Jack lets her in. They both walk into my living room where I am sitting in tears, to tell me they are sorry and they didn't plan for this to happen. Isn't this rich? The new kid on the block, that I extended a welcome to and befriended, has just come and stole my husband. I ordered them both out of my house, to never call me or come to my door ever again! Now they get to walk off into the sunset and enjoy what they've done while I have to tell my son your dad has left us for a neighbor. My son is a sweet, 13 year old young man whose day is about to be ruined when I decide to let him know what's going on. I sit here, numb and in total shock at how things worked out.

1 month later

Jack comes to my house asking to come in. Reluctantly I let him in. I was still hurt but I did miss him. We sit down at the kitchen table and he begins to tell me how he wants to work things out. He agreed to go to counseling and focus on getting a job. I tell Jack I don't think things will work out being that the person who came between us lives two doors down. He pleads and cries about how he's truly sorry and he's done with Renee. We have sex and agree on trying to work things out. Jack then runs back over to Renee's house, gets his things and moves back home. Everything is going well for about two weeks and then boom a problem. He started creeping with Renee again. I caught them in bed at her place again so I kindly put all Jack's stuff on her doorstep. I have had just about enough of his false promises. Jack talks a good game but he cannot follow through at all. He wants to live the life of a player, so it's time for him to man up and get a divorce. I am ready to say game over and call a lawyer.

Once Jack and Renee came up for air, she noticed his belongings on her doorstep. She was more than happy to bring his stuff back into her place. At this point things began to get a bit hostile. They were celebrating for a while but then Renee started getting tired of taking care of Jack. Common sense lets her know if he cheated on me while I was working, he just may do the same thing to her. Renee demanded that Jack get off his ass and go get a job or else. That didn't work out so well. Jack began knocking on my door and making up excuses to see me. He even began coming to my job and taking me to lunch with money, he got from Renee. I rather liked this shoe being on the other foot thing. After while Renee was getting hip to what may be going on and followed him where he was meeting me. She borrowed a friend's car so he wouldn't recognize he was being followed. Thirty minutes after we were in the room, there was a knock at the door. Like a fool,

Jack answers, and it's Renee. She storms in the room as if she has a right to be mad at a husband and wife being intimate. I am at a hotel with my damn husband and his mistress barges in as if she's the wife. All I could do is crack up because this was just ridiculous. While she was screaming at the top of her lungs at Jack, I was sitting there with a smile on my face. Then I got up, collected my things and walked away. For the life of me, I can't understand why I keep subjecting myself to this nonsense. I love my husband and I want to work things through but he's not ready. In my heart of hearts, I knew that staying in competition for his affections with Renee was just enabling him. We keep making this monster bigger and more powerful. Renee was ready to back down and I wasn't ready to let her win just yet. It was time to come up with a plan to end all the drama.

I ignored Jack for about a month and then finally called him over to be with me. I heard through the grapevine that things weren't going well between Renee and him. This is the perfect time to strike and put my plan in motion. I sweet talked Jack and made all types of false promises. We made love to seal the deal and while he was asleep, I slipped out of bed to Renee's. That side door is open, but I was sure to wear gloves so I wouldn't touch the door handle. I found Jack's liquor and sprinkled poison in it. Closed the bottle back nice and tight and got out of that house and back home. I was sure to slide back in bed beside Jack before he woke up. Thirty minutes later, he hopped up and said he was heading back to Renee's. Jack promised he would end things with Renee tonight over dinner. He was so excited, I told him I was pregnant and he just melted like butter. Once again, he made many false promises because I knew his weak flesh wouldn't allow him to behave. Jack wasn't one to fight the temptations of his flesh, he just went with the feeling. Oh, to be a fly on the wall in Renee's kitchen tonight. Fireworks will be popping off like crazy! She is going to be angry tremendously and ready for some serious revenge. I almost feel sorry for the poor saps!

Shortly after 6pm, all you hear is a lot of screaming and yelling coming from Renee's house. The kitchen window was cracked so you can hear them fighting. He must have told her the good news of our little one to come. She began throwing Jack's clothes out the front door and threatening to kill him. Neighbors were watching from their windows and front doors. Jack was screaming at her from outside and then next thing you know he collapse. I immediately rush out to his side and scream for someone to call 911. The ambulance and the cops came. They questioned the neighbors and took Renee down to the station for questioning. I told the police they were fighting because Jack was leaving her to come back home to me. Right away, this will go down as a crime of passion. Fortunately, Jack didn't die but he came close to it. Renee got an attempted murder charge and had to go to jail. Jack went to rehab for his drinking issues and I pray he gets help with that cheating problem as well. As for me, I'm living happily with my son. I finally got my divorce and I am free of Jack and his drama. I have learned that I can be neighborly but not to friendly, and to stay out of other people's home. You can visit every now and again but not daily or weekly, unless you want problems. Now Renee has more neighbors than she can handle. I wonder whom she's sleeping with now? I can guarantee you it's not someone else's man, unless she's screwing the prison guards. I hope you've learned something after reading this but if you didn't, let me remind you. Stay away from married men, and don't be a home wrecker, because you just may find yourself in prison for attempted murder.

PENELOPE'S PRISON

My name is Penelope Henderson and life has been truly hard for me. I still have terrible nightmares of my days imprisoned. My horrifying nights and days of starvation. People say love is blind but they forgot to add crazy as well.

I was a charismatic young woman when I first met Jefferson. There wasn't a soul I came across that didn't enjoy my company. I am a people person, always have been. I have a great sense of fashion, style, and I am business savvy. I was always on point with current events and I can talk shop with the best of them. I work and play hard but I love even harder. When I love a man, I give him my all and there's nothing I won't do for him. I am loyal to a fault and I wear my heart on my sleeve. That is my biggest downfall. Love is my weakness and the right, evil person can exploit that. Jefferson was that perfectly evil person; a master manipulator at its best. Jefferson has the smile of an angel and the soul of Lucifer. O' how I wish, someone had warned me of men like this. Jefferson's touch can make you shiver with pleasure or tremble with the greatest fear. You could say he was a modern day Dr. Jekyll and Mr. Hyde.

I thrived in the business world and Jefferson loved that about me, so I thought. While we were dating, he treated me like royalty. Bahamas for lunch, Paris for the weekend, and Monte Carlo just because we can. I love life with Jefferson, it is magnificent. Who would have thought that this gentle giant could be such a tyrant?

Jefferson had alienated me from my family and most of my friends. Brainwashed me into thinking that I didn't need anyone else but him. He convinced me that everyone is so envious of our life together that they will do and say anything to break us apart. My parents and my brother told me that I was changing and I had become distant. Jefferson had my head so big with compliments I could float away like a hot air balloon. After while I stopped hearing from my family. I imagined they were tired of dealing with my diva attitude and just left me alone. My pride got the better of me and I didn't bother reaching out to them. Who did they think they were? Don't they know I am Penelope Barnes? People want to be me so who are they to reject me and ignore me? I'll show them!

Now, we are at a place where Jefferson talks me into retiring and being a homemaker. He feels as though I need more time to tend to our home and him. The brainwashed fool that I am does just what he asks of me. Anything for my dear Jefferson, who has done so much for me over the years. The only one who hasn't turned his back on me. The only person I had left in this world. Oh, he did a number on my brain. He fills your head with so much nonsense as he pleases you sexually to keep you under his spell. Jefferson is at the top of his game when it comes to pleasing a woman sexually. I would do whatever it took to keep him happy so I wouldn't be deprived of my pleasure. I was a slave to his touch. A mere lap dog of lust; if he told me to get down on my knees and beg for it, I did. Jefferson was my addiction of choice, and I became a full-blown junkie!

Eventually, the things Jefferson wanted became more outrageous. This one night he came home with this sexy lingerie set for me to wear. Complete with six-inch high heel shoes and a mask. I am freshly showered because I knew he was coming. I took the lingerie set into the bedroom, put it on, and waited for Jefferson to come into the room. He came in the room and to my unpleasant surprise, a woman accompanied him. Immediately I raise my eyebrows as to what the hell he was thinking? This woman had on this Cleopatra type attire. She has a caramel color complexion as if she just arrived from Egypt. She is tall, shapely, attractive, and exotic. Jefferson is extremely taken by her; I can tell by the way he was drooling. He whispered a few words in her ear and she began to walk towards me. Cautiously, I watched her every move and I had my guard up. Jefferson tells me to relax and let her have her way with me. I screamed are you crazy? I am not into threesomes Jefferson! He came toward me with an angry look in his eye, and grabbed me by my hair with force. He whispered in my ear to do as I am told or else. I have never seen this side of Jefferson before. I was a bit frightened and angry at the same time. I had to let this woman do whatever she wanted to me while Jefferson watched with pleasure. I was sick to my stomach and when it was all over with, I had to vomit. I was in the shower for what seemed an eternity. I felt so dirty and ashamed. This is the very day I began to dislike my husband. I am baffled; this is not the man I married. I cried until I couldn't cry anymore. The room became a blur and I fell off to sleep.

I awake to the smell of delicious food. Jefferson comes in the room with a tray full of yummy things to eat. There were pastries, fruit, waffles, bacon, a cheese omelet, fresh squeezed orange juice, and milk. He placed the tray across my lap and kissed me good morning. He tried to give me this heartfelt apology about how he didn't mean to hurt me last night when he pulled my hair. I just smiled at him and didn't say a word. I didn't know what would happen if I expressed my opinions on how I felt about things. I wanted to let him know that I am not into women or threesomes. The nerve of him, to insist on putting me in a very uncomfortable situation.

A week went by and Jefferson didn't touch me, he barely spoke to me. He came home with the scent of another woman's perfume with lipstick on his collar. Tonight I demanded to know what is going on. He tells me to sit down and be quiet. That I had no right to question a man about where he's been and with whom. I screamed at him, like hell I don't! You are my husband and you owe me an explanation damn it! His breath oozed with liquor and his tongue with venom. Jefferson kept his back to me while I was demanding an explanation. Finally, he swung around and the look in his eyes is pure evil. Almost as if, he lost his soul. He grabbed me by my neck and forced me up against the wall banging my head. He was yelling, telling me how ungrateful and disrespectful I am. Before I knew it, Jefferson dragged into the basement. I'm kicking and screaming like a mule but he orders me to be quiet before he kills me. I know he is serious about killing me so I stop screaming. He flicks on a light and I see a wall with chains and other gadgets. My heart is racing with fear. Jefferson chained my hands and feet. I am bound and gagged. He's rattling on about how I've been a bad girl and I need to be punished. Tears stream down my face while I am shaking my head as to beg him to please don't do this. I couldn't reach him no matter what, Jefferson was gone and this animal was in full control. He ripped my clothing from my body and then took his belt from his pants. He whipped my bare body until I had whelps all over. He even beat my breasts. My body goes into shock after awhile and I am numb. I pass out from the pain and exhaustion of it all. A shooting pain brought me back. Jefferson forced his penis into my rectum and he had anal sex with me. He was so rough I began to bleed from my backside. I cried so hard and long. The sweat burned my badly beaten body and I am as helpless as a newborn. Jefferson finally stopped, walked back upstairs, and closed the door behind him. I was so glad to be alone at that moment. I cried out to God like never before. I wanted my parents so badly. I fell to sleep after about 3 hours and when I awoke, it was another day. Hours had went by and no sign of Jefferson. I am hungry and so thirsty by now. Another day goes by and no Jefferson. I gather he's out of town on business and left me here to die. I need a shower, I can smell myself and the stench is terrible.

I hear the doorbell ring but I can't scream for help being that I was gagged. After ringing the bell a few times and knocking, the person went away. I hear the heavy vehicle pull away; I believe it was a UPS truck. I'm sure it's the dress I ordered online from Sax 5th Avenue. If Jefferson keeps me down here much longer, I will need a smaller size.

Another day goes by. My stomach is growling so loud it would scare off a pit bull. I have a headache bigger than Texas and I smell like the city dump. I begin to cry out to God in prayer once more. I can recall the scripture that says; I can do all things through Christ who gives me strength. Then I can hear the words, God will never leave you nor forsake you. I can hear my mother say, be strong in the Lord in the power of his might. Just then, I hear footsteps. I didn't know if it was Jesus coming for me or Jefferson. It sounded to be about three people in the house. The cellar door opened and two big men were dragging a limp body down the stairs. To my surprise, it was Jefferson getting dragged, but one of the men who were dragging him looked exactly like Jefferson too. My eyes leaped open with shock and confusion. The two men held Jefferson up and turned on the light so he could see me in this terrible condition. A look of terror and remorse was on his face. Jefferson got a jolt of strength and began to run towards me. One of the men shot him in the back and Jefferson fell at my feet. I screamed but no sound came out. I am so scared and confused and begin to pray. All of a sudden, I see shadows of big bodies, the house begins to shake, and the two thugs run out of the house as if they saw ghosts. The cellar walls shook so hard that the chains came out of the wall setting me free. I was still so weak that I fell to the floor and crawled over to Jefferson. He managed to get himself up off the floor and help me over to the stairs. We both had to just about crawl our way back upstairs. Jefferson called 911 and explained the situation. While we were waiting for them, I begged Jefferson to put me in the shower. He refused and told me I would wash away evidence. He told me his brother was behind all this because he was envious of how his dad left him the business and not Johnson. He told me how he was a hostage in his Brother Johnson's basement for about a month now. All that time I thought it was Jefferson manipulating me.

I know two things for a fact, Jesus is real and he shows up right on time. I thought I was going to die in that basement and that I lost my husband forever. I thank God for helping me through this terrible ordeal. I called my family and let them know Jefferson and I were both in the hospital and we would need their help. As for Jonathan and his accomplice, someone in the prison is returning the favor for what he did to me. It took a little time for my body to be free of any signs of a beating. Jefferson recovered well from his gunshot wound and we are closer than ever. Our families come around more and we are getting better and better with time. I thank God for all things but I am most thankful for my salvation and being set free.

LIVING A LIE

Do you know what it's like to live a life of lies? To tell yourself day in and day out, he loves me he just doesn't know how to show it. Yes, he cheats all the time but he always apologizes and buys me flowers and a gift. Let's not forget, I know he hits me but he doesn't mean it. I make him too angry, set him off, and he lashes out at me. He's always so sorry afterwards. He even cries and tells me he doesn't mean to hit me he just can't help it. I know if I could just control my mouth a little better and not make him so mad he won't hit me anymore. Moreover, the alcohol turns him into a monster. If he didn't drink he would be so much nicer. I know I can help him change because I love him and he loves me.

James and I have been together for 7 years. We dated for two years and proceeded to get married. The first three years of our marriage was great, but by year 4, things began to change. I had begun to notice a change in my husband. He is somewhat distancing himself from me. At this point, I figure it was time to sit down and see what is going on. Did I put on a few extra unwanted pounds, are my looks fading, maybe I'm not sexy enough in the bedroom. What did I do to cause this gap in our relationship? Why is it that, as a woman, we always take on the blame? We always assume that it's something that we've done wrong or something we are not doing? Right away, it's always our fault that things aren't working out the way they are supposed to be.

Tonight, I was going to get down to the bottom of the drama. I made James's favorite meal; filet mignon with a fresh steamed vegetable medley and a baked potato. I went to Red Lobster and ordered a dozen of their delicious cheddar bay biscuits because I love them! I put a bottle of sparkling cider on the table and smooth jazz on the radio. It was a lovely spring breeze dancing with the blinds against the window. You can smell the flowers in bloom and a small hint of spring rain in the air. This will be the perfect night for romance and reconnecting as a couple. I showered and put on my sexiest little black dress. I spray on a little Burberry Weekend perfume in all the right places. Just a small touch of make-up, he likes a natural look. Okay, I am all set and ready for James. He should be walking through the door in five minutes tops. James arrived everyday at 5:15pm like clockwork. It's time to light the candles and greet him at the door. Quarter after five and I'm at the door with a smile on my face, but James doesn't walk through the door. Okay, maybe there was some traffic today so he's running a little late. After twenty minutes passes, I am a bit antsy and concerned. I grab the phone and call his cell phone to see what's holding him up. The first five times I called, he didn't pick up so by now I'm almost frantic. I dialed him two more times and by call number 7, he finally answers. He gives me this song and dance about a friend of his is going through something and he's out with him. I scold James for not calling me earlier to let me know because I was worried. I also told him I had something special planned for us tonight and that he should hurry home as soon as he could. He kind of blew me off and rushed me off the phone. He didn't even say I love you or ask me what I had planned for us. When James finally walked through the door, it was 10:15pm and I am wrapped up in the fetal position on the sofa. He turns on the light to reveal the table setting and the food I prepared. The candles are burning to the bottom by now. I deliberately let them burn so he could see how long he had me waiting. He tapped me on the shoulder and began apologizing for keeping me waiting so long. James told me how his friend Lionel is having financial issues and problems in his marriage. Being that James is a finance consultant, he claims he was helping Lionel make a budget and a plan to get back on track.

I sat James down and asked him straight out, why are we so distant from each other lately? You barely spend any time with me and we haven't made love in weeks. What's going on with us James, I am concerned? I am almost in tears because this really affects me deeply. James apologizes and says he hadn't noticed the distance. The workload and trying to stay afloat of everything financially for us and his clients is just taking a toll on him. James vows to be more attentive and spend more time with me, starting tonight. He warmed up dinner; we eat and talk while sipping our sparkling cider. It felt nice and we stayed up talking until about 1a.m. We ended the evening on a positive note. We made love and fell asleep in each other's arms and I felt safe again. Every woman needs her husband to be her safe place.

2 Days later

Another man has come and gone and James is back to being his inattentive ways. He has been coming home late every day from work. James claims he's been working overtime to help his firm manage the case load being that two consultants were fired. Fine, I can understand that and I don't give him any grief about it. I have been keeping busy reading new books, doing yoga, and trying new recipes. James's family comes out of Tennessee so I want to try to surprise him with a little southern cuisine tonight. Deep-fried chicken, cornbread, potato salad, yams, red beans and rice. Everything is just about done and I'm ready to fry the chicken. The deep fryer is filled with oil and hotter than the equator. After the first 5 pieces begin to fry I feel somewhat light headed and nauseated. Next thing I know, I'm running to the bathroom and barely made it before vomit came rushing forth out of my mouth. What a time to get a bug. I get myself together, brush my teeth, and go back to monitor the chicken. I'm not sure if James will be home on time tonight or not but dinner will be ready either way. The cornbread, yams, and the beans and rice smell heavenly. I sampled a taste of the potato salad and that was good. I am so proud of myself at this moment. My first southern meal and it came out great. I am following the recipes out of a book titled, Sylvia's Family Soul Food Cookbook. I finish frying the chicken and set it in a bucket filled with paper towels to drain any excess oil. I am excited and can't wait to see the look on James's face when he sees the meal I prepared for him tonight! He will be pleased, I'm sure.

James comes in the door at 5:30pm. The food is still warm and my appetite is rearing to go. As he comes up the stairway and heads towards the kitchen, I greet him with a smile and welcome him home. James sniffs the air and immediately asks if his mom is here? I giggle and tell him of course not, that I have been working all day to make him a real southern meal. He swept me up in his arms and spun me around like a wild man. We both giggled like children and raced to wash our hands to eat supper. I made our plates and we enjoyed the food and each other's company. James face is alive as he speaks about

Tennessee and his family. Living on a farm with six other siblings must have been a blast. I had an older sister but she died in a fatal car accident when I was 10 years old. My parents were heartbroken. Julia planned to attend Harvard Business School and was at the top of her class. Such a bright future she had ahead of her until a drunk driver took her away from us. I miss her so much it's been fifteen years since she's been gone.

I could tell something was weighing on James's mind by the way he looked when he entered the house earlier. He's been putting in overtime like crazy at work for the last month. I felt as if he did it to avoid being around me. Maybe I was wrong, there could be something else going on. Whatever the problem, it was put on the shelf tonight. James and I talked and laughed as if we didn't have a care in the world. We fell asleep on a blanket in the living room on the floor. James's alarm went off at 5:30am to get him up for work. He jumped up and ran to the shower. I picked the blanket and myself up off the floor and went back to bed in our room. To my surprise, I awoke to find James bringing me breakfast in bed. That was the biggest shock. He hasn't really been this attentive towards me in ages. At least not until after he's slapped me around a bit. He thanked me for last night's dinner and conversation. I didn't know what to say, I was speechless. I just smiled, said you are welcome, and wished him a great day at work.

I enjoyed my breakfast and sat in bed for twenty minutes; thinking could this possibly be things changing for the better? I have been praying and wishing that things would be normal again. This is as close to normal as it's been in so long. I had to walk on eggshells constantly with James. You didn't know what to expect from day to day with him. One minute everything is fine and the next he's grabbing you by the hair and banging your head against the wall. I was petrified of James but I loved him just the same. I guess you can say he was kind of like Dr. Jekyll and Mr. Hyde. I wanted to leave many times but he threatened to hunt me down and kill me. He also threatened to harm my parents, and I truly believed that he would have done it. He had so many different personalities. He was fine when he wasn't drinking or dealing with some of the hard knocks life throws at us. James is not a man who is good under pressure. No matter how much I would encourage him through hard times, he just didn't have enough faith for himself.

Time to get up out of this bed, clean up the mess in the kitchen, get showered and dressed, and start my day. As I start walking the tray towards the kitchen I feel a little light headed and nauseated. I'm guessing I have a 24 hour bug. I guzzle down a glass of water but immediately it comes rushing back up, along with breakfast. I run to the bathroom, after cleaning the kitchen sink thoroughly, to brush my teeth. I shower, put on some fresh pajamas, socks, and head back to bed. I didn't have a fever but I felt fatigued and weak in the stomach area. At this point, all I want to do is take a long nap and wake up refreshed. My nap continued to be interrupted by frequent trips to the bathroom to pee. The more I drank to stay hydrated the more I had to urinate. I finally got a solid nap in but when I finally woke up it was 5:35pm and James came in the bedroom yelling. Screaming where in the hell is his dinner. At that moment, I knew it was going to be a bad night. I jumped up and tried to explain to him I had a virus and was in bed most of the day. James immediately accused me of being a lazy, lying, and no good whore. He asked me if I had a virus shouldn't he have the same virus. I guess he had a point but I couldn't explain why he wasn't feeling as awful as I was. I can tell he's been drinking, I smell it on his breath and see it on his countenance. As I confront him about drinking, he tells me to stay out of his business. I then ask James what went wrong to make him fall back off the wagon. He really lost it after that. He shoved me so hard I flew backwards over the nightstand and hit my head on the headboard. Reality has just set in. Yesterday and this morning was just a temporary moment, the real James is back in the building. I felt faint while getting up off the bedroom floor. I put my hand on my head and felt the knot rising up fast. As I pull my hand out of my head, I see blood on my fingers and I then faint. James turned back to yell at me some more and at that point I was already falling back on the bed. He saw the blood on my hand and I'm guessing he called 911 because I woke up with EMT's standing over me. They were taking my blood pressure and asking me questions when I opened my eyes. One of the men told James to take me into the ER to get my head scanned to make sure there was no head trauma that they couldn't see. James was in no shape to drive anyone anywhere and I didn't want him near me either. I called a friend to take me to the ER. I didn't even have to explain why I didn't want James to take me, she already knew about his violent outbursts. This wasn't the first time she's had to take me to the emergency room.

After being there for a while I found out I didn't have a concussion or any head trauma, but I tested positive for pregnancy. My jaw dropped to my neck when the nurse told me I was pregnant. My girlfriend Jennifer had mixed emotions about it. She was happy for me but afraid for me at the same time. Jen knew that James's violent ways could really hurt the baby and me. I guess I wanted to be in denial about that because I was elated about being pregnant. That sure does explain all my lightheadedness and fatigue the last few days. The nausea and vomiting was there because someone is occupying some residence up in my womb. I placed my hands on my flat belly and smiled with joy. I got the okay to go home so I quickly put my clothes on and couldn't wait to tell my mother. On the way home Jennifer told me, she's happy for me but she warned me to be very careful. She also told me not to be surprised if James isn't as happy about the pregnancy as I am. I didn't even stop to think that maybe he wouldn't be happy, but she was right. What if he isn't as happy about this baby; is he going to try to kill us both in an angry rage? I don't want to jump the gun and just jump straight to the negative. Maybe, just maybe he might be just as happy as I am.

When Jennifer dropped me off, I went inside the house to find it a mess and James nowhere in sight. Where could he be and it's after midnight? I proceeded to clean up the mess. There was broken glass, shattered frames, and pillows tossed all over the dining room. Alongside the sofa, there was vomit on the carpet and it smelled awful. I had to run to the bathroom and vomit myself. I cleaned up as much as I could with paper towels and then shampooed the carpet. After getting everything cleaned up, I fell into bed and immediately went to sleep. When I awoke, it was 10a.m. and still no sign of James. I must admit, I was glad he wasn't around to ruin my morning. I had fruit and cereal for breakfast, got my shower, and relaxed on the sofa watching television all afternoon. Around three, I felt a strong craving for cheesecake so I got dressed to go out and get some. I asked Jennifer if she would like to join me for an early dinner at the Cheesecake Factory. She agreed so we went and had a great time. I had steak, a baked potato, some steamed veggies, and lemonade for dinner. Of course, I had the strawberry cheesecake afterwards. We went inside the mall and browsed a bit. I purchased a new nightgown with matching robe and slippers. I peeped at the baby layette; I couldn't resist and had to take a look. Soon after we headed back home and James's car was in the carport when I pulled up. I looked at my watch and saw it was 7:15pm. Time flew by today while I was out. Once I got inside the house, James met me at the door and snatched me in by the arm. He screamed at me where have I been all day. Before I could even answer, he accused me of being out with another man. He snatched my packages, saw the satin nightgown, and went nuts. In his mind, I purchased this for my lover. He smells like a brewery and looks like the devil himself. He slapped me across the face and demanded I tell him who I was out spending time with. I screamed, James please I wasn't out with another man now stop it. He shook me until I threw up at his feet. He finally let me go. I screamed, please James stop it! Don't hit me please, I am pregnant! He looked at me as if he had seen a ghost. His face ran cold and went pale. His eyes almost jumped out of their sockets. He grabbed his keys and wallet and ran out of the house. I just stood there as he bolted out the door. All I could hear was Jennifer's words: James may not be as happy about this pregnancy as you are. At this point, there's only one thing left to do, pray to God for a miracle. I got down on my knees and cried out to God. I pleaded and made all types of deals with God if he could just change James's heart. I loved my husband but I hated his ways with a passion. I needed James to talk to me and confide in me, as a spouse should. He has always treated me like an outsider when it came to his inner most demons. I know he's fighting and trying to escape something and he turns to the bottle instead of God. I was determined to believe that underneath that mean, bully, abusive exterior there has to be a heart. I am waiting for the day that he gets his heart of flesh and throw away the heart of stone. God please help James before it's too late. Although I am praying for James, I am in need of prayer myself. Only a fool would continue to stay here with him and his violent ways. I really thought I was helping by standing by him in the midst of these violent outbursts but it's really doing more harm than good. I guess it's time to stand on my own two feet and let James work out his issues on his own. If I didn't want to do it for myself, I had to do it for this baby. I didn't want my child to grow up in a house of violence, but a home built on love and grounded in God. I am determined to give this baby the best life I have to offer him or her, starting with leaving this chaotic situation.

It seemed like an eternity waiting for James to finally come back home. I fell asleep on the sofa after the first two hours. I decide to get up, brush my teeth, wash my face, and make something to nibble. I cut up some fresh fruit and grabbed a bottle of water out of the fridge. It's really going to be hard to get through to James if he's not in a sober state of mind. God please let James be sober when he arrives because I really need to reach the heart of him. Our child cannot live in a house that is not a home. As I munch on a piece of cantaloupe, I hear a car pull up in the driveway. Okay it's James, get ready girl a lot is riding on the outcome of this conversation.

James enters the living room with flowers, candy, and a card in hand. He must have cleaned up at his office. He is freshly shaved with a haircut and the biggest smile plastered across his face. This right here has me baffled but curious to see what will happen next. James walks over to the sofa, gets down on bended knee, and apologizes. Part of me was so happy but I had enough sense to know this is just for the moment. Been here and done this with James so many times before, I am not a fool any longer. As he gives this heart-felt apology, I cry inside and out, he really thinks he means this. James is only fooling himself because I am a true believer that he needs help and I cannot give it to him.

James: Why are you crying Lori? I am apologizing to you, I am sorry for mistreating you the way I have. I know I stormed out of here yesterday but I'm back now. I'm better baby and I'm so happy about us having a baby together.

Me: James, I truly thank you for your apology honey and I know you think you mean it but we've been down this road before baby. I love you James, more than you could ever know but you need help. You need to get back in AA and try to work through your issues of life. You are angry five days out of seven and you've become more abusive.

James: Lori, I am fine I just had a rough couple of weeks from the pressures at work but I promise baby, I'll do much better from now on. I will cut back on my drinking and come home on time and everything.

Lori: James, my darling James if only you knew. Baby, you really need to stop drinking altogether not just cut back. You are an alcoholic and a mean one at that. Your words are cruel and your hands are vicious. You have hurt me emotionally and physically repeatedly, and they all came with apologies and flowers afterwards. I cannot and I will not allow you to hurt this baby the way you've hurt me over the years. I think you should see yourself from the outside looking in for just a moment. Come take a walk in my shoes a while. Think about how you've mistreated me and hit me. How you don't trust me and constantly accuse me of being with other men. I try to be the best wife I know how but it's never enough for you James. I was working you had me quit to be home to tend to you and your needs full time. I gave up being me and who I am to be who you wanted me to be. That's not love James, that is control. I don't want to be controlled like a horse or a machine James; I want to be loved beyond measure. I want to be treasured and treated with respect and value.

James: I can do that, all that and more Lori if you just give me a chance. I love you, Lori truly I do. I know I have to try to let the alcohol go before it destroys me. I want to learn to be the kind of husband you need in your life. I want to be a great father to our child if you just allow me to be Lori. I swear baby, I won't hurt our child and I will get help.

Lori: James, I know you want to be a great father and I know you wouldn't hurt this child intentionally. I'm sure you will get help with your addiction and blossom into a great man. You will learn and become a great husband but for someone else, not for me. Our journey together has ended James. You are either a lesson well learned or an assignment from hell, but whichever the case it is finished. My heart is breaking because I truly love you James but I love me too. I cannot exist in your world.

James: Lori no, you cannot leave me, not now baby! I need you so much right now Lori; like never before. Please baby, I'm here on my knees in tears begging you, please forgive me Lori! Stay with me damn it!

James threw the flowers and candy across the room. The anger began to well up within him. I looked at him with tears of sorrow in my eyes, walked away towards the bedroom to pack my things to go. James stayed in the living room and began pacing back and forth. I knew he was trying to think of a plan on how he could get me to stay. At this point, there was nothing he could say to make me stay another day. When a woman is fed up and has her mind made up, there is nothing you can do to turn her around. Today is that day for me, I am out of here. As I head down the hallway towards the kitchen, James runs ahead of me blocking me. He's ranting and raving about how he cannot live without me and he refuses to let me leave. I pull out my cell phone and threaten to call 911. He moves out of my way and lets me walk a few more steps before grabbing me by the arm. He yanks me backwards and threatens to commit suicide if I leave him. I pulled my arm away and kept walking. As I was about to put my foot on the first step I hear James running towards me full speed ahead. I turn and get out of harm's way and next thing you see is James tumbling down the steps and out of the window headfirst. I screamed like a mad woman and called 911. I went outside to see if he was conscious and still breathing and he was. I got down on my knees beside him and let him know the ambulance is on the way. It was a messy sight before my eyes. He had glass sticking all through him and bloody all over. He managed to muffle out a few words.

James: Lori, I am so sorry for all the pain I have caused you over the years.

Lori: Sshh...don't try to talk James, save your strength baby. (Lori cradles James's upper body in her arms)

James: Lori, please let our baby know that I love him and don't let him know what a monster I was. Only share the good parts of me with our son. (James holds Lori's hand to his heart)

Lori: You are going to show him that you are capable of being a good man and not a monster James, just hang on help is on the way. James please, I love you! Just hold on. Silence was all I heard and then I screamed James and shook him. He opened up his eyes again and blood came out of his mouth as he tried to speak once more.

James: Lori, I love you and please know that you were a great wife and every day I was proud to come home to you. I know I messed up a lot but this baby is the one thing I did right. Let's name him Richard after my grandfather, he was a good man and not a monster.

Lori: Yes James we can name him Richard. If it's a girl though we may have a problem with that name. A little girl will not like to be called Richard.

James: Don't worry it's a boy, I can feel it in my heart and he's going to be handsome and strong. He will bring you so much joy and make you proud. I can see it already. (James smiles as he imagines his son as a young man)

Lori: I am sure he will, he will bring us much joy and we will be so proud. The ambulance is here now James, we're going to get you help right now.

James: I love you Lori and please be happy and find love. (James squeezes Lori's hand one last time, smiled at her, and took his last breath)

EVERY WOMAN'S NIGHTMARE

I thought Charles and I were happy. I mean sure, every couple has its share of vicissitudes but we didn't have many bad times. We may have had a good argument about two or three times a year but nothing serious. Charles never laid a hand on me in a violent manner. The first few months of dating, he didn't pressure me into having sex with him. He was very patient and loving with me every step of the way. Not once has he ever called me out of my name, thank God because it would have been dangerous up in that house. You can call me mean, bossy, even disrespectful at times but never make the mistake of calling me a bitch. When a man takes it there, that means he has lost all respect for you and it's time to go. My dad told me when a man could stand before you and call you the "B" word his level of respect for you is down to none. Things are never the same after that. I know things are said in the heat of the moment out of anger and after the cool down period, you wish you could take it back. We've all been there and done that, no doubt.

Anyway, I begin to notice Charles taking on a lot of overtime work. Soon he would have to go out of town on business. Charles worked in Pharmaceuticals. He would take new medicines and introduce them to hospitals and doctor's offices. At first, I didn't really question it and I let him go about his business. Then I start to notice his sexual appetite and behaviors begin to change. One minute he doesn't want to be touched and he's cranky, the next he's happier than ever, but only after these out of town business trips. I didn't question him about his mood swings or the lack of sex, I just sat back and took notice of all the changes. I then decide to do some damn investigating. I had to wait until his next out of town trip to find out what is really going on. I called his secretary, Janice, to ask her to give me his schedule for the next two months. I told her a little white lie so she would keep this between her and me. I fed her a story about wanting to set up a romantic rendezvous. Janice was very helpful and excited about helping me plan. She called the Ritz-Carlton in Philadelphia and added me to his hotel reservation so I would have access to a room key. I thanked Janice for all her help and got her a pair of tickets to a Broadway show. She gave me a gift and I blessed her with a gift in return.

Time for me to go over my schedule and make sure I have those two days free and clear. I do most of my work from home. I am a corporate lawyer. I enjoy what I do but I'm really ready to step my game up to another level. Maybe broaden my horizons to criminal law; although there are plenty criminals in these big companies. Money laundering and all types of shady things go down in big corporations.

Anyway, I have two weeks to get my work done and in order. Then take a two-day break. Tonight I will go online and see what Philly has to offer, other than a great cheese steak and the Eagles. Charles's schedule just came through via fax from Janice. I wanted a copy to go over and have for myself. When Charles gets in and we sit down to dinner, I will ask him about his work schedule. I'll ask him when will he have a day or two off so that we can have personal time for us. I will let him know I have been feeling kind of neglected the last few weeks and how we need to reconnect. Which isn't a lie because he has been quite distant lately. He even had the nerve to use the old, I have a headache not tonight line on me a few times. It took everything I had in me not to slap his teeth out of his mouth. I don't know exactly what's going on with our marriage but I do know what's not going on. I keep myself looking good on a daily. Hair, nails, eyebrows, and make-up stay on point. I have a body that's lean and sexy. My smile is inviting and my teeth shine, no cavities here. My gums are pink and healthy. I have breasts, a slender waistline, and a toned shapely butt. I get my feet done once a week, so they are never rough. My pedicure is always in check. My hair is shoulder length, but to spice things up at times I will put on a wig. I am not cutting or coloring my hair, but I will improvise with a wig. Sometimes I will wear a strawberry blonde, shortcut wig. It's like a Halle Berry cut. I remember one night I put on a sexy red wig, tapered cut and formed to my face. I wore a sexy black leather bodysuit with matching stiletto boots, gloves, and a whip. I spoke in a French accent and modeled for him. All he could say was I have a presentation to work on we will have to play naughty French girl another time honey. He barely looked up from his laptop before sending me on my way. I'm sure his work wasn't that interesting that he couldn't put it down to play with me for a while. At that point, I just stopped trying to get his attention romantically. I get compliments and invitations from all types of men on a daily basis when I am out handling my business. When a woman isn't wanted at home and being wanted everywhere else, trouble is not far off. Reading your bible all the time and going to church twice a week isn't always enough to keep your flesh under submission, when temptation is always riding shot gun in your Bentley. Human beings need love, affection, compassion, and a comforting touch. You can only go so long without it before you slip up. For those who think they are too saved to fall into temptation, you better go back and read your bible. The only one who can never be tempted and never fall is Jesus Christ. Everyone else is subject to mess up somewhere along the way, if you are not careful. Everyone wants to feel loved and special. Am I right? If you agree just say, amen sis! ☺

(Two weeks later)

Charles thinks I'm going to be in San Francisco on business this Thursday and Friday. The other night when I asked him if he would be free to fly out with me he told me he couldn't. Now that's all well and fine, but when I asked him about his schedule things didn't add up. Now mind you, Janice already let me know he is scheduled to be in Philly this week, but he told me he had to be in Chicago. He even showed me an itinerary and the whole nine. Now I'm really curious as to what the hell he's up to. I never questioned Charles about his business schedule. Whatever he told me, I just took him at his word. I just kiss him good-bye and tell him to say hello to Oprah for me. I jump in my limo and head out to the airport. I made sure my flight was booked and gone two hrs prior to his arrival at the airport. When I arrive in Philly, a car takes me to the Ritz Carlton and I take an adjoining suite to his room. Then an hour later, I put on a wig, some dark shades, and go back to the front desk and get the key to Charles's suite. I go in and plant my little cameras and taps around the room. Technology these days, it's a blessing for some and a curse for others.

When Charles arrives, I am sitting in the lobby in a disguise. He indeed comes in with a blonde woman. I couldn't see her face, just the back of her head. At first, I was ready to jump out and stomp him! Then my smart mind said, hold up, she may be a client. I sat back and waited to see what would happen next. The bellman took Charles's bags up to the suite but Charles and the blonde-haired person headed to the hotel restaurant. They have a glass of champagne and talk a while. The blonde person than excuses herself and heads towards the powder room. I follow her right in there to get a closer look. I purposely knock into her to make her drop her purse. After apologizing for bumping into her, I help her retrieve the items that fall out of her bag. I noticed she had some big hands and didn't look very feminine. She was definitely an ugly female. I asked her if she was a Philly resident because this was my first time here and wanted some recommendations of dining and entertainment. She said she was here on business and wasn't from Philly so she didn't know much about what it had to offer. I wished her a wonderful day and went out shopping for tonight. She was hideous and I knew Charles definitely wasn't romancing her. I am off to go buy some new perfume and sexy lingerie. I will get a massage, a facial, a manicure and a pedicure.

After my shopping and spa day, I am relaxed and ready to treat Charles very nicely. I felt bad about thinking the worst about him and that woman, but he lied about what state he would be doing business with today. That right there would raise an eyebrow on anyone. I didn't know what I would say to Charles tonight. I relax in my suite a while and fall off to sleep. When I awake, it's about two hours later. I jump up after I peek over at the clock. I rush to the shower to get refreshed and hop out. I dry off, touch up my makeup, perfume my body, and slip into my new lingerie. I take a quick last glance at myself in the mirror before heading towards the door that adjoins Charles and my sweet. I hear smooth jazz playing on the radio through the door and I smile. It sounds like he's definitely in the mood for love, so I slowly and quietly unlock and open the door towards Charles's suite. I walk in and head towards his bedroom. I see women's clothing on the floor, heels, and a blonde wig. Now I'm ready to cut up and act a fool because this fool is up in here with that ugly ass blonde thing! I get to the bedroom door and open it slowly so they won't hear. What I saw next was enough to make a woman commit murder! As I stand in the doorway of Charles's bedroom suite, my blood runs cold as my heart stops. My world is shattered as I am rocked to my core. Charles, the 1 who met me at the altar before God and many witnesses; promised to honor and cherish me just dishonored our love in the worst way. My Charles, is wrapped up in bed, with another man violating our vows and God's law. I felt so sick and I begin to vomit right there on the spot. Charles and his lover stop in their tracks when they finally see me. They were both caught off guard and the look on Charles's face was priceless. The looks of pain and anger radiated from my face and Charles froze in shock. He couldn't even say my name. The other man ran and began to grab his clothing to leave. I told him, please don't leave on my account, I'm just Charles's wife and I ran out of there as fast as I could. My heart pounding like a jackhammer, and my head spinning like a top I fell upon my bed and wept. I couldn't get the image of that abomination out of my mind. I am so glad Charles didn't know what suite I was staying in so he couldn't come looking for me. There was nothing left to say but good-bye. I didn't want his excuses nor to hear his sob story. All I want is a divorce and to be HIV free. So many married women are popping up HIV positive behind their in the closet husbands. Why can't these people stand up and be honest about their sexuality and what they really want? Why must they hide behind marriage and an unsuspecting woman who falls in love with them? I truly thank God we did not have children and I have no further ties to this man. I know God is with me because I could have gone crazy and tried to kill Charles, but instead I walked away. I left him and his perverted ways behind and never looked back. Charles didn't fight me on the divorce or any of the settlement agreements. He knew I despised his lifestyle and the only thing I felt for him was pity. I prayed that God would come into his life and help him see that he was sick and needed God's help. When I received the final paperwork for our divorce decree, there was a letter from Charles attached by a paper clip. He attempted to contact me via phone calls, emails, and text but I didn't answer any of them. I guess he figured I would open the divorce papers and I would see the letter. At first, I refused to read it. For the first two weeks it just sat on my desk underneath a paperweight. The following weekend I finally sat down at my desk with a cup of coffee and began to read Charles's letter. It explained how he was sorry that he didn't deal with his sexual issues before we got involved. He truly didn't mean to hurt me and that he does love me in spite of him wanting to be with a man. Charles felt ashamed because he knew it's not normal for a man to lust after another man and lay with him. He wasn't ready to deal with the battle he was fighting on the inside so he tried to live like a normal man. His fleshly desires were more powerful than he was. Charles let me know he did not have aids and he used a condom every time he had sexual relations with men and me. He apologized and hoped that one day I could forgive him for hurting me. What Charles didn't know, is that I forgave him a while ago. As a child of God, I know what he requires of me. We must forgive so that we may be forgiven in return. It's not always an easy thing to do, but it's a must.

KEISHA'S SECRET LIFE

I married at a young age, despite my parents' warnings and concerns. You couldn't tell me anything because I was in love and I knew it all. I was determined to get out of my parent's home and start life on my own, by any means necessary. I was so sick and tired of hearing, while you are under our roof you will abide by our rules. I wanted to live my life and have fun sometimes. I was sick of being the only one in the eleventh grade with a 9:30 pm curfew.

During my senior year at high school, I thought about maybe going to the Navy or something. All that changed when Larry came along. He was an older man; he had a job and his own place. I met him in October, right at the beginning of senior year. In my mind, I was a big deal because I'm the only girl in the twelfth grade who is dating a man. All the other girls were dating eleventh grade or twelfth grade boys. Some were having sex, but not me; I was making love, so I thought. When the girls got together and spoke about their liaisons it was nothing compared to the things Larry and I did. Just the thought of his touch made me weak. He had a kiss that would make your clothes fall off immediately. Besides being a great lover, Larry was very intelligent. He spent most of his time with his nose in a book. He had a wall of books in his living room at home. He wore glasses and looked very studious when he read his books. Larry made me want to be a better student. He helped me with my homework and with studying for my SAT's. My grades were better than ever! My parents took a liking to Larry because of his intelligence and the way he pushed me to do better in all things in my life. Of course, they didn't know he was twenty years old and had his own place. My mom would have put an end to that relationship immediately. They figured he was a senior as well. When they asked him what he was going to do after graduation, my heart leapt up into my throat. I was wondering how he would talk his way out of this one. Then I thought, what we are going to do when June arrives and they don't see Larry on the graduation program. That is definitely going to cause major problems. I had to find a way to tell my parents about Larry's age but I wanted to wait until my 17th birthday.

It's now Valentine's Day week and I wanted to plan something special. My best girlfriend Lisa and I went to the mall and grabbed a few sexy items for the occasion. I purchased a pink sheer, ruffled cami with satin straps and bows. Matching pink open front panties, with a ruffle back and side ribbon ties. I also purchased a cute eye mask and stiletto heels. I wanted to have a Burlesque look. I put on a sexy, short cut wig and long fake nails. I planned to make this a night Larry would never forget. I planned to use hot candle wax, whipped cream, handcuffs, and a whip. Lisa looked at me as if I was crazy. I gave her a look as if to ask, what's wrong with the items I plan to use? Lisa told me she was somewhat concerned about me. I told her she shouldn't knock it until she tried it. Lisa and Robert were only into the traditional things. She's never even been on top before. She let Robert do all the work. I asked her if he has ever gone downtown on her, and she seemed shocked by the question. I asked if she's ever pleasured him with oral sex and she nearly gagged. I thought to myself, man she's missing out on a lot of pleasure. I told Lisa to insist that Robert pleases her with oral sex and live a little. Her eyes got big, but she was somewhat curious when I told her about my experience. I told Lisa that it's instant gratification and how it made you shake uncontrollably with pleasure and moan with delight. I told her she would squirm like a worm in hot ashes and want him to devour her. If you are going to have sex, get the maximum pleasure out of it, don't half step! Curiosity is written all over Lisa's face. I can tell she is eager to see what it's like. I was excited for her.

A few months have gone by and it's now May. Next month is graduation and I still have not told my parents that Larry is a grown man. He is a student, but a student in college and not high school. My heart jumps at the thought of telling my mom. She is truly going to be pissed and ready to strike like a cobra. Girls can somewhat pull on their dad's heartstrings but Mother's are a bit different. They are strictly business when it comes to discipline. My mom will see this as betrayal and banish me to my room until I'm 21 years of age.

My tummy feels so nauseated and my head is spinning. I'm so excited and looking forward to leaving childhood and entering into adulthood. I can move in with Larry and start a new life with him as an adult, his woman and his lover. It's going to be so wonderful! We'll wake up in each other's arms every morning and have breakfast together. It's going to be great and I cannot wait. I already know when my parents' find out about Larry's age the first thing they are going to say we forbid you to date him any longer. Then they will go into their as long as you are living under our roof you must abide by our rules. That will be my cue to say I can respect that and I am moving out right now. I can't wait to see the look on their faces when I say that; it's going to be priceless.

GRADUATION DAY

A few of my best girlfriends are over my house and we are taking photos in our caps and gowns. Everyone is all smiles and excited. This is our last day of high school, praise the Lord! We have a short break before school begins again, but it's a whole different ball game. College is not going to be a cakewalk like high school. Assignments will be longer, harder, and worth more per grade. Your courses will be harder and the time to do them will be shorter than high school. I will have to focus and be more determined than ever. I'm sure it's going to be exciting as well as challenging and rewarding when I have my degree in my hand.

My friend, Mercedes, just asked me if Larry and I told my parents the truth about his age yet. I told her we're going to tell her after graduation because I didn't want to ruin things before the ceremony. Larry wanted to tell them earlier but I wasn't ready to deal with the fall out during the school year. I wanted to keep my happiness and my GPA at a great level. I truly enjoyed my senior year to the fullest. High school years are supposed to be a great time in life and I can truly say this year was a great one. I can't complain because senior year was awesome!

It's time to head over to the school for the graduation ceremony. On the way, my parents asked where Larry was and why he didn't come over for photos. I told them he had many things to do and that we would take photos afterwards. Mercedes and Lisa look over at me with a nervous look in their eyes as we approach the school building. My dad let us out in front before he parks the car. I make my way over to the crowd of my fellow students and embrace them. I quickly find Larry and take a few photos with him as well. I let him know that I would be telling my parents the truth today after the ceremony. A look of relief came across Larry's face; I thought that was strange because I was very nervous about it.

It is now 7pm, time for all the graduates to take their seats on stage and get the ceremony started. I am so excited about getting my diploma! In just a few minutes, I will be a high school graduate. I thank God because years ago African-Americans weren't able to receive an education. This is truly a proud day for my ancestors as well. With a smile, I think back on great women like Harriet Tubman. What she endured I couldn't have been that strong! How she rose above her circumstances and helped others out of their situation. She risked it all to help others; nowadays people will barely lift a finger to help you. It's truly sad how human beings has lost the humanity within.

My name is called; I rise up proudly to receive my diploma. I look over at my parents with a smile and then Larry. He blew me a kiss and my heart smiled. When the final student received their diploma, my heart jumped with fear. It's now time to deal with the matter at hand.

My parents looked baffled because Larry didn't walk across the stage and receive a diploma like everyone else. Here comes the drama. I walk towards my parents and Larry joins me out of the crowd. I felt like I was taking a walk down death row.

Mom: What happen, why didn't Larry receive his diploma? You are very intelligent so we know you didn't fail any classes.

Larry: I will be receiving my degree next week from the University. I am a senior in college.

Dad: What the hell is going on here Keisha? Let's take this conversation to the privacy of our own home. This is not the time or place for this discussion.

The ride home was a silent one. My mom's face let me know that this was not going to be easy. The look of disappointment masked her face and the scent of betrayal filled the car. Boy did I feel sick to my stomach. The garage door rises and dad pulls in. I run into the house because I feel the vomit rising up in my throat. Afterwards I brush my teeth and rinse with Scope. I get myself together and join my parents and Larry in the parlor.

Mom: So, what else have you been lying to us about Keisha? You know every time I try to convince myself that I can trust you, you pull a stupid stunt like this!

Dad: Hold on now Eileen, let's go about this in a more calm tone of voice. Don't get your pressure up honey.

Larry: Mrs. Haney let me start by saying I am truly sorry and I told Keisha from the beginning that she should be honest with you and your husband.

Mom: Larry, you are the adult in this, you should have been the one to open your mouth. Keisha is just a kid and you are a grown man! Why didn't you open your mouth? Don't try to ease out of it by saying, o well Keisha didn't want to tell you.

Dad: Son, we allowed you in our home and welcomed you into our lives. Why did you betray the trust we had in you? I feel like you really manipulated Keisha, my wife and me. Give me one good reason why I shouldn't knock you on your ass right now?

Larry: Sir, you have every right to be angry and I am sorry. There is no excuse to help the situation. I hope you know that I do care for your daughter.

Mom: Do you respect our daughter Larry?

Larry: Yes, I have plenty of respect for Keisha, Mrs. Haney.

Mom: Okay, let's see. Have you been intimate with our daughter Larry?

Keisha: Mom, that is personal!

Mom: Keisha, sit back and be quiet because I am two seconds off your ass little girl!

Larry: With all due respect, I really don't feel comfortable discussing my personal life with you.

Mom: Larry, with all due respect, I really do not appreciate you taking advantage of my young daughter sexually. I think it would be best if you just get out of my house now before someone gets hurt!

Keisha: Mom stop it! Larry wait, don't leave. Mom I love him and I don't plan on breaking things off with him.

Mom: Keisha, it's not up to you. You will do as you are told and I forbid you to see Larry. Your father and I have brought you up better than this. You know that God is not pleased with the way you are doing things. If Larry had any respect for you, he would not have allowed this lie to go on this long. If he truly cared for you, he would not have manipulated you into bed before marriage! Wake up and smell the coffee girl!

Dad: Keisha go upstairs to your room! Your mom and I need some time to talk and figure out what we are going to do with you.

Keisha: No, I will not go to my room! I'm not a little girl anymore daddy! Hello! A high school graduate standing here! You're treating me like I'm in pre-school! You all are standing here discussing my life as if I'm not even in the room. I will not go to my room and I will not stay silent! I love Larry and I will not break things off with him!

Mom draws her hand back and slaps me across the face. Larry and Dad's eyes get big with surprise. I should have known that was coming after I said that to my mom. I don't know what I was thinking. At that moment, I grabbed Larry's hand and stormed out of the house. My dad called out to me several times but I left and didn't look back. I was embarrassed and angry. How could she slap me like that in front of Larry? I asked Larry to get me out of town for a little while. I wanted to put as much distance between me and my parents as possible right now. We all needed time to cool down and gather our thoughts. I knew the first place my parents would go looking for me is Larry's place. I called Lisa and Mercedes and let them know my secret was out about Larry's age. I gave them the low down on how everything went and ended. I also informed them that I would be gone for a few days and my mom would be calling them to find out where I am. I didn't want to put them in the middle of things by telling them my whereabouts, that way they won't have to lie to my parents.

The first night out, we spent at his parents' home, about an hour away from town. We explained the situation to them and that's when Larry's mom asked him and his dad to leave the room. Mrs. Jamison wanted to speak with me privately.

Mrs. Jamison: From a mother's point of view, I can understand how your parents are feeling. You led them to believe that Larry was indeed a high school student. He went along with it so that really makes him look bad as a man in your father's eyes. Before you blow up at them, put yourself in their shoes honey. You outright lied to them and you flaunted it in their faces every time you brought Larry into their home. They trusted you and Larry so this indeed was a slap in the face. As a woman in love, I can understand your position. Love can make us do foolish things sometimes. Yes, you were wrong for keeping Larry's age a secret but he was equally wrong for going along with it. Had I known, I would have demanded he go to your father like a man and tell the truth. You both should have started things off the right way because now it's going to be difficult for your parents to believe anything you two say.

Keisha: Mrs. Jamison If I would have been honest my parents probably would have forbid me to see Larry. I couldn't take that chance. I love Larry and he makes me happy. I want to build a future with him. I know they would have gotten in the way of things, I just know it.

Mrs. Jamison: Yes, any parent would have reservations about their young daughter dating a grown man. Larry has more experience with life and that can easily put pressure on you to do things you are not ready to handle. For instance, if you're a young virgin and you fall for an older, experienced man the pressure to sleep with him will be greater than dating someone your own age. Being sexually active is not a game and it shouldn't be taken lightly. When you make love for the first time, it shouldn't be something you regret shortly after. Usually when young girls give themselves to a man, it's because they feel they love them. Most of the time it's just sex to him. Men go by sight and women by emotions. You may be in love where as the man is just enjoying your body. Young people think they know it all and don't want to listen to their elders. That is where you go wrong by being hard headed. Many times, I wish I had listened when my mother or grandmother tried to school me on a few things in life. Parents love their children and we try to spare them any pain when and where we can. Unfortunately, we sometimes have to stand back, watch our children crash and burn, and be there to pick up the pieces in the end. I love my son but I can't support him in wrong doing. Lying to your parents about this was indeed wrong Keisha. I can't make you do anything, but I will tell you this; your parents love you honey. Go home and work things out before things get out of hand. I'm sure you all said things out of anger and have some hurt feelings, but get pass that. When it's all said and done, your parents are always going to be there when the dust settles. A man's love is sometimes conditional and limited, but a parent's love is forever and unconditional. Just because your parents have rules, regulations, and limits to what they allow, the love is limitless. If you walk away now and never fix things with your parents you will indeed be sorry honey, trust me.

Keisha: Thanks for listening and talking with me Mrs. Jamison. I heard everything you said and I will work things through with my parents. I'll see if we can talk things through tomorrow with cooler heads and less anger.

2 DAYS LATER

It's time to face the music and deal with my parents concerning the Larry situation. I walk in the house and my dad is sitting in his recliner reading the paper. My mom is in the kitchen making dinner. I say hello to my dad and give him a sincere look. He knew I felt horrible for walking out and staying gone for two days.

Dad: Welcome back runaway graduate! Connie, the prodigal daughter has returned home. Give your poppa a great big hug little girl.

Keisha: Oh daddy, I am so sorry for the way things went down. I didn't lie to hurt you, it's just that I knew you guys wouldn't let me see Larry if you knew his age.

Mom: You got that right. Keisha you are too young to be involved in a serious relationship. This is a time in life when you should be thinking about a career and your future. For some reason, when a young girl gets so involved with these older guys their dreams and goals are put on the back burner. I don't want that to happen to you Keisha. You are too bright to spend your youth tending to some man's needs and wants. You haven't even lived the best part of your life as of yet. These young men today are only interested in getting the goodies free. Why should they marry if they are getting all the benefits without putting a ring on your finger?

Keisha: Momma that isn't the case here. I don't have to compromise my career or dreams. Larry supports me in what I want to do. He is in favor of higher education and women being financially independent.

Mom: That's all well and good Keisha, but how does he feel about abstinence? What's his take on waiting until you are married to have sex? Is he in favor of that?

Keisha: Mom, Larry didn't force me into doing anything with him. I did what I wanted to do with no pressure from him.

Mom: Oh my goodness, were you at least careful and safe? Did you use protection every time Keisha? STD's and AIDS are real! I'm sure they taught you about that in health class.

Keisha: Mom, I understand that you feel disappointed and betrayed by Larry and I but that's not what this is about. I didn't tell you and daddy because I knew you would try and force me to break things off with him. I love Larry, he makes me happy and I want to be with him! Can you accept our relationship mom?

Mom: Keisha as a woman of God I cannot condone your carrying on with this man. I understand about being young and thinking that you are in love. Your hormones are raging out of control and you just run with it. Those very hormones can bring about more trouble than you can imagine. You have your whole life ahead of you sweetheart. Why are you in such a rush to be an adult? Trust me; it's not as easy as it looks.

Dad: Listen to your mother honey. We love you and just want the best for you. From a man's point of view, I can tell you that Larry isn't as honorable and noble as you think. For starters, he wouldn't have let you come here and deal with this alone. Larry has a bit more experience with life than you do little girl. When it comes to manipulating young girls, older men know the tricks and the words to say. I know right now you think I'm just saying this to make you second guess Larry but that is not the case. Keep your eyes open and your mind clear. Think back and go over everything that took place from the moment you met. Can you honestly say Larry didn't initiate a sexual relationship? Was it really all your idea? The last time I checked you wanted to be pure for your wedding day. So many things have changed about you since you've started seeing this young man. Your mother and I, we don't know this new you. The new Keisha, who lies and sneaks around with a grown man behind our backs; we don't know you.

Keisha: Daddy look, I know you just want me to stay your little girl forever but I can't. I have been growing up for quite some time now and it only continues. I love you daddy and I'm sorry I have disappointed you and mommy but I'm only human. You guys are acting as if you don't remember what it's like being my age. I know parents don't want to think about their daughter's starting to be intimate but it happens daddy. Larry sees me as a beautiful young woman and you see me as your little girl. He didn't force me into doing anything, I was equally ready. I know this is hard to hear because it's hard for me to discuss this with you.

Mom: Thomas I don't know about you but I know for a fact that I will not condone this lifestyle. I love you Keisha and I only want the best for you. Right now, you really don't know what's best for you because you seem to be blinded by other things. You do know that God is not pleased with what you are doing and there are consequences and repercussions to follow. It's best that you repent now and turn from this sinful way Keisha. Trust me, the sooner the better honey. Right now, you are a young girl playing an adult game and you don't know all the rules my darling.

Keisha: Mom I know you love me and you are concerned about my well-being but I'm happy with Larry. I don't plan on leaving him. I am not going to stop seeing him anytime soon. I know how you feel about things, where you stand, and I can respect that. I only ask that you do the same for me. The only solution to this problem is for me to move out. I don't want to disrespect you and your household so I'm going to move in with Larry.

Dad: Keisha are you out of your mind? You barely know this young man! Shacking is against God's law and it will only end badly. You're not ready to move out on your own yet. You just graduated from high school, what's the rush?

Keisha: Daddy, this is the only way things will work. I love you and mom and I don't want us to keep hurting each other. I'm not going to change my mind and I know you guys aren't going to accept my decision. There's nothing left to say or do but leave. I am so sorry for disappointing you daddy, so sorry.

At this point, I am heart broken by the sadness in my dad's eyes. I wrap my arms around him and squeeze tightly. I hate that I hurt him so badly. I turn to hug my mom and she has tears in her eyes as well. She gave me a hug and then walked back into the kitchen. I went upstairs to pack and I called for Larry to come pick me up. I took my luggage and went out on the porch to wait for him. He was shocked to see me waiting for him with my luggage.

Larry: What the hell is going on Keisha? I thought you came home to work things out with your parents, not run away from your problems. You are making matters worse between your parents and me. We never discussed you packing up all your stuff and moving in with me. I am not ready for this type of commitment Keisha!

Keisha: Well I didn't discuss getting pregnant at an early age either, but I am! So if you're not ready for this type of commitment Larry, you better get ready!

Larry: Pregnant...oh my goodness, I am nowhere near ready for all this! I have a future planned Keisha and this will just ruin it all. This is bad, really bad! The timing couldn't be worse. I am moving; my job has promoted me to a better paying position. They are relocating me to Boston. I cannot put you and a baby on my insurance, we're not even married.

Keisha: When were you planning to tell me about this big move Larry, after you got off the plane in Boston? You have some nerve you bastard! Unbelievable, my dad was right. You are just a grown ass man taking advantage of a young girl!

Larry: Hold up Keisha! I didn't take advantage of you. Not once did you turn down any sexual advances, hell you initiated most of them. I almost felt like you were using me for the sex! I also felt you used me to get under your parents skin. This was never about loving me; it was about sticking it to your mom and dad!

Keisha: Are you serious right now Larry? I was a virgin and I gave myself to you out of love! This child is growing out of that love, so I thought! You don't love me Larry?

Larry: I didn't say that Keisha, I do love you but I just wasn't ready for moving in together this soon. Then adding a baby to the mix, this is a lot to drop in my lap. This is all happening so fast. I am not financially set to take care of a family right now Keisha.

Keisha: Well Larry I understand what you are saying but I am a Christian, we don't do abortion! It's against God's way. I already made the mistake of indulging in pre-marital sex. Being a fornicator was the first wrong move, but the flesh is weak. I have prayed and asked God to forgive me for my sins. I want to start over and do things right in the eyes of the God I serve.

4 Months Later

I'm at my parent's front door to break the news to them. Larry and I are getting married and having a baby. Talk about killing two birds with one stone. They are not going to be happy about this at all. I haven't really seen them in the last four months so I'm sure mom will be happy to see me. I ring the bell and my dad let me in with a smile. He asked why I didn't use my key. I let him know being that I moved out I don't have the right to use the key. My mom was sitting out on the deck enjoying a glass of iced tea with lemon. As I walked out on the deck and she laid eyes on me, she dropped her glass. My mom knew immediately that I was pregnant but my dad didn't notice. At that moment, I felt so ashamed. I tell her before she gets all upset and her blood pressure rises that Larry and I are getting married. I didn't want to dishonor God any further. My stomach wasn't huge but she could see the pregnancy in my face. My dad was shocked and speechless. I know he wanted to strangle Larry if he could just get his hands on him. My parents asked why Larry didn't accompany me and have this talk with them. Larry was at his parent's place telling them our plans as well. My parents are not happy about me being a wife and mother so immediately out of high school. This was not the order of my planning. I thought I was going to have a career first and kids later. Unfortunately, life takes its own path whether you're ready for it or not.

My dad asks that we all bow down together before the Lord in prayer. When things begin to get a bit tough, my parents always turn to God in prayer. That helps, especially when tempers are flaring. Prayer sets the atmosphere for the spirit of God to come in and work things out for your good. Everything worked out for me with my parents. I am sure things went as well for Larry and his parents.

A few days later, we all meet up at the Justice of the Peace for the ceremony. When Larry and I were on our way back home to Boston, I felt at peace. My life was now in order and pleasing in the eyes of God and man. Yes, I am young and pregnant but I'm married so no one can say anything! I'm married with a baby on the way. These words weren't planned to be coming out of my mouth this early. Maybe ten to fifteen years from now after I've had a career. I really don't know how this is going to play out. I plan to keep God in the midst of the whole thing though. He's the only one who can make it right. I am putting all my faith and trust in God. No matter what happens, I know it's for my good.

6 Months later

Lisa and Mercedes are up for a visit to see the baby and me. Larry and I decided to name her Isabella. Everyone called her Bella for a nickname. I was so excited about my baby girl and having my dearest friends around. Things haven't been so hot between Larry and I. He adores Bella but he didn't look at me the way he used to. I'm guessing things may get better after I get my pre-pregnancy body back. I wasn't huge and sloppy, just needed a little toning here and there. I shared my concerns with Lisa and Mercedes, but they told me I might be feeling ignored because of the baby. They tried hard to reassure me that it was all in my head and Larry was in love with me. I appreciate them for trying but no matter what, I know what I felt. When your man has lost interest in you, you are the first to know.

For the next two months, I began to work out faithfully. I ate only salads, lean meats, veggies, beans, and yogurt and drank water. I really became focused on building myself back up because Larry sure wasn't helping. The distance between us grew but my waistline was slimming down. My stomach toned with each passing month. When I took Bella for walks in the park, I noticed men glancing my way again. It felt nice to be looked upon again, just wish it were Larry and not strangers.

Bella will be 1 years old next week, and I decided I was going to go back home and have her surrounded by family. We don't know many people here in Boston so it would just make sense to go home for this occasion. I booked a flight for Bella and myself, but I didn't inform Larry of my plans. I kept my distance from Larry, only made conversation when asked a question. I kept our interaction to a minimum. I was going to show him just what it feels like to be ignored.

My pre-pregnancy body is back and in full swing! I put on a nice, little black dress that flattered my figure. It wasn't to clingy but it fit nicely. Even Larry had to take a second glance this morning before leaving out to work. I had my make up on and my hair looked great as well. Bella was dressed to impress as well. Larry made a comment on how lovely daddy's girls looked this morning. He even kissed us both on the forehead before walking out the door. I bid him a good day and continued with my plan. Bella and I had a plane to catch at ten, so I headed out by seven. A limo service picked us up and dropped us off at the airport. My cell phone rang at eight thirty; it was Larry calling to my surprise. I let the call go to voicemail because I didn't want him to hear all the commotion in the background. He left a message asking if Bella and I would like to join him for lunch today. How ironic is that? I've been dying to spend time with Larry and the day he decides to make time for me, I don't have time for him. Life is funny that way. Being neglected over the last year has really turned me away from any romantic feelings toward Larry. I love him but I don't trust my heart in his hands any longer. I have learned to be content with just taking care of Bella and building myself back up. Larry's lack of appreciation and total ignorance has made me stronger than ever. Going back home and being amongst my family and friends will benefit me greatly. I will truly see how I would like to proceed concerning my marriage. Larry will have time to himself to think about what he wants as well. I can't work on this marriage by myself. If he's not willing to meet me half way then we are truly doomed. Larry is a great dad and he adores Bella but he is truly lacking in the loving, attentive, caring husband department. He's always so busy when it comes to our relationship.

Time to board the plane and I cannot wait to see my parents. I called them last night and let them know Bella and I would be coming down for a visit. I guess Larry's parents will find out when I stop over with Bella for a visit. I must admit I cannot wait to find out Larry's reaction about this. I haven't been able to get a rise out of him any other way. I'm sure this will definitely get his attention!

Our flight was brief and my parents were there to meet us when we came through the gate. It felt so good to see faces of people who were actually happy to see me. Haven't felt that way at home in ages. Larry always seemed to be disappointed to see my face when he came through the door each night from work. I remember there was a time where he couldn't keep his hands off of me. Now he doesn't touch me at all, unless it's by accident. If any of his body parts touch mine in bed it's because he rolled over in his sleep. That didn't happen much because he would wrap up like a pastry puff in his blanket. At times, I would just giggle inside because little does he know by this point I didn't want him touching me either. You can't make love with having love to begin with. Maybe we built our relationship on lust and it was never love from the beginning.

After getting in the car and on the road to my parent's home, I turned my cell phone back on. I had two voice mails and one text. They were all messages from Larry asking where am I and why haven't I responded to his lunch invitation. I sent him a text message back informing him that Bella and I are out of town and we could not join him for lunch. Furthermore, he would be on his own for dinner and breakfast tomorrow as well. O boy, after I hit send I couldn't help but smile inside. I gave Bella a high five, as if she knew what was going on. I started discussing Bella's birthday plans with my mom and dad. My parents wanted to go to a fancy place to eat but Bella's only one years old. I figure we could do something simple at the house with a few family and friends. A nice cake, finger foods, beverages, and tons of photo taking is all we need.

My cell phone began to vibrate and I already knew it was Larry without even looking at the caller id. I let the call go to voicemail because I knew that would irritate the hell out of him. I checked the message shortly after. He was asking where I am with his daughter and I shouldn't have left town without informing him. I sent a text message back telling him Bella is fine and he never cares to know any other time where the hell I go. My cell phone began to vibrate again and again I let it go to voicemail. I know that he's steaming right about now. He left a voicemail and sent a text message demanding that I pick up my phone immediately. I just looked at the text message and rolled my eyes. You don't demand me to do a damn thing, I'm not your child! I sent him a text message back informing him I cannot talk right now and I would speak with him later.

We were in the driveway of my parent's house and I could hear the house phone ringing through the kitchen window. I bet that's Larry calling them trying to see if they have heard anything from me. I'll be sure to delete his number off of the caller id box before they see it. My dad already asked me if Larry would be joining us for Bella's big day. I told him I wasn't sure because Larry's job is unpredictable these days with when he would have to be out of town on business. My mom said it would be a shame for a father to miss his baby's first birthday. I did start to feel a little bad once she said that. I guess I can let Larry know where I am so he'll be able to see Bella on her first birthday.

We get in the house, put the luggage up in my room and I put Bella down for a nap. I then join my parents for a tall glass of iced tea with lemon and conversation. My mom has done a few renovations in the den and in my dad's office. After fifteen minutes has passed I go to check in on Bella. She was still sleeping so I took that time to call Larry. Here we go with the drama. Am I ready for this conversation? I guess I have to be at this point.

Me: Hello, you wanted to speak with me.

Larry: Keisha, where are you? Where did you take Bella?

Me: Bella and I are fine Larry. I felt like seeing my parents and friends so I flew home.

Larry: Why couldn't you just say that in the first place Keisha, I mean really! You do the craziest things!

Me: Larry please! Since when did you start caring where I am? You barely even say two words to me when I'm home so don't act like you care now! Like I said, Bella is fine and we are here at my parent's home. We will be here for a while.

Larry: Well what is a while Keisha? How long do you plan to try to keep my daughter away from me? You know her birthday is in two days?

Me: Larry stop with the dramatics! I'm not keeping you away from Bella, you know where my parents live. Yes I know her birthday is in two days and I'd rather her celebrate here amongst loved ones. We don't really know anyone in Boston so it would be best if she had her first birthday around family. Both sets of grandparents are here so it makes sense.

Larry: That's all well and good except for the fact that you're wasting money on flights, that I really can't afford right now.

Me: Well don't worry, I didn't spend any of your precious money to get here. Your funds are still intact and in case you haven't noticed I haven't asked you for a dime in ages. I pay the bills and get groceries and that is it.

Larry: If you were in need of something you should have asked, I can't read your mind.

Me: Larry please a real man knows when his woman is in need. You know I need a few dollars; I don't have a job right now. You can play the nut role if you want. The bottom line is you really don't give a damn what I'm in need of. I've been in need of a husband for months now and you can't even do that. No my mistake, you can but you choose not to be! I'm sick of it! I had to get out of that house before I lose my mind. I needed to be around a loving atmosphere so Bella could see what a real home should be. What we have in Boston is a joke, not a home. I have had enough. You want to walk around and act like I'm not even there. Well you got your wish; I'm not there so rejoice Larry! You finally have your place to yourself! You are Keisha free baby! Enjoy, I'm sure you will sleep really well tonight because I will not be in your bed.

Larry: Keisha what the hell are you talking about? When I get home from work, I'm tired and I may not be up for long conversation but I do acknowledge you.

Me: Well gee thanks Larry! Asking me if there's any mail or messages for you is not quite talking. You are so full of it. As I said, keep playing the nut role but you're going to have to play alone because I'm done! Game over baby, you win!

Larry: Woman please, I'm not playing the nut role! You're the one acting crazy, packing up our daughter and leaving without saying anything.

Me: You know what, I'm so done with this conversation Larry. You know where Bella and I are. If you decide to see her for her first birthday this is where she'll be.

Larry: Wait a minute Keisha; I'm not done talking to you.

Me: Oh now you want to talk to me. When I'm right in front of you in Boston you have nothing to say. You know what Larry, why don't you just send me a text.

Larry: Would you please stop acting so childish and listen!

Me: Larry, I do apologize for packing up Bella and just flying home without informing you, which was wrong of me. Other than that, I have nothing more to say to you at this time. I'm going to hang up now okay? You have a great day and take care now.

Larry: Oh, it's like that now? Okay Keisha I'll see you soon and don't try to hop another flight somewhere else to keep Bella away from me.

Me: I wouldn't dream of it Larry, good bye.

I know he is probably sitting there in his office wondering what just happened. This was a long time coming, and I hate the fact that he's sitting there as if he doesn't know what he's been doing. He's been ignoring me and avoiding me as much as he possibly could. Maybe it's time to just face the fact that our time as husband and wife are up. Probably shouldn't have happened in the first place. Getting married just because you are having a child together is not a good thing to do.

Larry made it to my parent's place for Bella's first birthday. His parents, my parents, and a few of my friends were there as well. Everyone had a ball but I'm sure they could sense the tension between Larry and me. I am glad Bella is too young to understand what we're dealing with. After all the company departed, we cleaned the dining room. I knew we had to deal with the elephant in the room soon. I'm sure our parents are wondering what is going to become of our marriage just as much as we were. I put Bella down to bed for the night then headed out with Larry. We grabbed coffee from Starbucks and really talked things through. I let him know how I was feeling inside about our marriage. I was so glad he didn't just sit there and act as if he didn't contribute to our problems. If he would've pulled that crap again, I'm sure he would have been wearing my cup of coffee. Larry let me know how right from the beginning the pregnancy and marriage was kind of thrust upon him. He felt as if he didn't have much of a choice or say so in the matter. This was somewhat understandable because he had planned things a bit different. He planned on going to Boston to build a career and become financially prepared for a wife and child in the future. He resented me in some ways for twisting his arm into doing things my way. As a Christian, I didn't want to be anyone's baby momma. I wanted to be a wife and mother as God planned for His children to live. I didn't take the time to think about how I was turning Larry's life upside down. All I thought about was how he is the one who got me pregnant and he's going to make an honest woman out of me. I admit that I resented him a little as well because I didn't ask to get pregnant, that was thrust upon me as well. Grant it a woman could choose not to keep the unexpected pregnancy, but not A Christian woman. Abortion is not an option for us. It goes against God and his law. In addition, I couldn't imagine killing an innocent baby. I don't have the lack of heart to do that. I knew life wouldn't be a walk in the park as a teen mom and wife, but it couldn't be all bad.

We both agree that Bella is the best thing in our lives and we couldn't imagine life without her. The question at hand is do we live without each other as husband and wife? If I don't bring happiness, love, and joy to Larry's world I'd rather leave it. I absolutely refuse to live as a neglected housewife. Women everywhere put up with a lot and we accept things that we shouldn't. The one thing you must take a stand on for your own sanity and happiness is to never settle for being a neglected housewives.

www.ingramcontent.com/pod-product-compliance
Ingram Content Group UK Ltd.
Pitfield, Milton Keynes, MK11 3LW, UK
UKHW040558210726
13854UKWH00008B/1387